AUSTRALIAN ARMY CAMPAIGN

# THE BATTLE OF

# FROMELLES

## 1916

# ROGER LEE

ARMY·HISTORY·UNIT

PROTECTING ARMY HERITAGE
PROMOTING ARMY HISTORY

2010

©Copyright Army History Unit
Campbell Park Offices (CP2-5-169)
Canberra ACT 2600
AUSTRALIA
(02) 6266 4248
(02) 6266 4044 – fax

National Library of Australia Cataloguing-in-Publication entry

| | |
|---|---|
| Author: | Lee, Roger. |
| Title: | Battle of Fromelles / Roger Lee. |
| Edition: | 1st ed. |
| ISBN: | 9780980658293 (pbk.) |
| Series: | Australian Army Campaign Series; 8. |
| Notes: | Includes bibliographical references and index. |
| Subjects: | Fromelles, Battle of, Fromelles, France, 1916. |
| | World War,1914-1918–Campaigns–France–Fromelles. |
| | World War, 1914-1918–Participation, Australian. |
| Dewey Number: | 940.427 |

Layout and design by Margaret McNally, Canberra, ACT
Printed in Australia by Big Sky Publishing, Sydney
Front Cover: Part of the German front line after the Battle of Fleurbaix which took place on 19 and 20 July 1916. AWM A01560
Title Page: Part of the German front line after the Battle of Fleurbaix which took place on 19 and 20 July 1916. AWM A01553

# CONTENTS

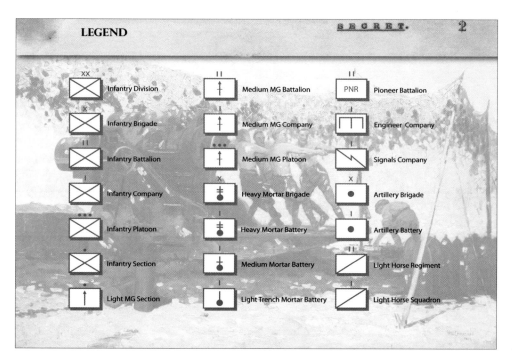

LEGEND    SECRET.    2

| | | |
|---|---|---|
| Infantry Division | Medium MG Battalion | Pioneer Battalion |
| Infantry Brigade | Medium MG Company | Engineer Company |
| Infantry Battalion | Medium MG Platoon | Signals Company |
| Infantry Company | Heavy Mortar Brigade | Artillery Brigade |
| Infantry Platoon | Heavy Mortar Battery | Artillery Battery |
| Infantry Section | Medium Mortar Battery | Light Horse Regiment |
| Light MG Section | Light Trench Mortar Battery | Light Horse Squadron |

# SERIES INTRODUCTION

In 2004, the then Chief of Army's Strategic Advisory Group (CASAG), the Army's senior generals, established a scheme to promote the study and understanding of military history within the Army. The focus was the Army's future generation of leaders and, from this, the Campaign Series was created. The series is intended to complement the Army's other history publications which are major analytical works of high quality, academically rigorous and referenced.

The Campaign Series focuses on leadership, command, strategy, tactics, lessons and personal experiences of war. Each title within the series includes extensive visual sources of information – maps, including specifically prepared maps in colour and 3D, specifically commissioned artwork, photographs and computer graphics.

Covering major campaigns and battles, as well as those less known, the Army History Unit and its Campaign Series provide a significant contribution to the history of the Australian Army and an excellent introduction to its campaigns and battles.

Roger Lee
Army Historian

# ACKNOWLEDGEMENTS

The first book is always a very steep learning curve for any author. This book was no exception and, during the long period of its preparation, I relied heavily on a number of people to provide ideas, support and, above all, encouragement. My colleagues in the Australian Army History Unit, especially Lieutenant Colonel Bill Houston and Dr Andrew Richardson, were always a source of advice and encouragement, with Andrew's computing skills often extricating me from one disaster or another. Professor Gary Sheffield, Major General Mike O'Brien, Major Dr Michael Tyquin and Mr Nick Fletcher all read early versions of the manuscript, offered many helpful and insightful comments and suggested corrections, thus sparing me much embarrassment. Any errors that remain are thus entirely my own. Craig Tibbitts at the Australian War Memorial promptly delivered material or advice on request and I owe much to Peter Barton and our many lively discussions on this battle. Indeed, some of his wisdom has found its way into these pages.

My gratitude extends also to the team of experts who have added so much to the book itself: Mark Wahlert for his maps and images, Jeff Isaacs for his wonderful artwork, Glenn Wahlert, the Project Director, for his calmness, patience and whip-wielding; and, of course, my patient, long-suffering editor, Cathy McCullagh. Margaret McNally was at her professional best with the typesetting and book design.

Finally, and not least, I must acknowledge and thank some others not connected directly with these pages. It is entirely due to the skill and persistence of oncologist Dr Paul Craft and surgeon Dr Charles Mosse that I am still around and able to write these words. While others may curse them, I am clearly in their debt. Last on my list but first in line for my gratitude is, of course, my wife Jenny, who has added to the English language a variant on the 'golf widow' and 'football widow' — 'damned book widow'.

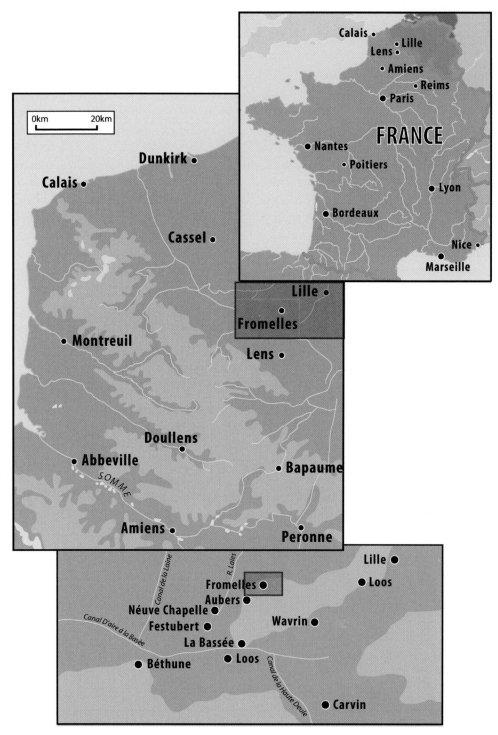

Location of Fromelles.
(Mark Wahlert)

# FROMELLES: THE BATTLE AND ITS STRATEGIC SETTING

## INTRODUCTION

At six o'clock on the evening of Wednesday 19 July 1916, the British 61st (2nd South Midland) Division and the 5th Australian Division began the attack that was to become known as the Battle of Fromelles. Within twenty-four hours, the 61st Division had suffered 1,547 casualties while the 5th Division had lost 5,533 men — a total that included over 1,700 dead or missing. In terms of total numbers, this remains the bloodiest twenty-four hours in the history of the Australian Army. There would be higher casualties in the battles on the Somme a few days later (but fought over a longer period) and with the surrender of the 8th Division in Singapore in the next war, but the catastrophic loss rate that characterised the Battle of Fromelles remains unsurpassed. Yet, surprisingly, there was little official recognition of the catastrophe at the time and, until recently, the battle was almost unknown outside the pages of the Australian *Official History*.

The focus of most history writers on the numbers killed or wounded has generated an understandable emotional revulsion against the whole experience of World War One. No historian debating arcane issues of loss rates is ever likely to overturn this natural and understandable reaction. Nonetheless, the total number of casualties is not a reliable pointer to the competence or incompetence of the commanders or the effectiveness of the defenders. The size of the casualty count is due almost entirely to the number of soldiers involved. The British Empire fielded the largest army in its history on the Western Front in 1916. Even a low casualty rate — that is, the proportion of casualties as a percentage of totals involved — still resulted in enormous numbers of dead soldiers.

The Battle of Fromelles had barely ended before the onset of recriminations. Eventually, after senior officers — including the commander of the 5th Australian Division — were replaced and other battles fought, the controversy ebbed and faded. The discovery in 2009 of the remains of 250 missing Australian and British war dead, casualties of the Battle of Fromelles, ignited a new wave of speculation and opinion. Unfortunately, in the more than ninety years since Fromelles, current opinion has often been influenced by ideas and issues notably absent on 19 July 1916. A number of myths and misrepresentations have evolved which distort understanding of what happened and do a disservice both to the soldiers who fought the battle and to those who planned and conducted it. Conspiracy theories concerning official British attempts to downplay the tragedy add little to the debate but have undergone something of a renaissance in recent times.

The bungling British general, a continuing and recurrent theme, has now become entrenched in popular perceptions of the war in both Britain and Australia. In Australia, Fromelles is increasingly advanced as a prime example of the result of such bungling. The more vociferous advocates of this theme frequently fail to demonstrate that their criticisms are based on an understanding of the nature of the battle, the options available to the various levels of command, or of the exercise of command in war. While the available evidence clearly shows that there was confusion, that mistakes were made and that the battle itself was among the most poorly executed by the British Expeditionary Force (BEF — the name for the British Army deployed to France and Belgium) that year, the reasons for these mistakes should be considered in the context of the strategic and tactical circumstances of the time. There are several fundamental lessons to be drawn from this battle, both in its planning and in the execution of the attack. In something as complex as a multi-divisional attack, no one person can ever be the sole influence on the outcome. Hindsight, the ability to draw on factors either unknown or imperfectly known at the time, or the use of factors over which individuals at the time had no control, should not be the basis for condemnation of the actions and decisions of specific planners or commanders.

## Fromelles Reinvented

The most celebrated biography of the Commander-in-Chief, Sir Douglas Haig, written by John Terraine in 1963, does not mention the Battle of Fromelles. A much more recent book on Haig by Gary Sheffield and John Bourne, however, makes several references to this battle. It is difficult to argue that Terraine was venting some hidden anti-Australian bias in ignoring Fromelles when his book specifically mentions all the other battles involving the Australia Imperial Force (AIF). The logical conclusion is that Fromelles had simply vanished from the story of the war. The recent interest among serious historians and enthusiastic Australian amateurs indicates that this obscure battle is being resurrected as a subject for research, something that can only enhance our understanding of the war.

Fromelles has become a standard-bearer for another emergent theme of the war. Writers and commentators in today's media accounts of the battle take great pains to identify soldiers as either Australian or British, as though this is somehow an explanation for the decisions of the higher command concerning their use or a reason for success or failure on the battlefield. While this distinction was and remains important to the question of a separate Australian identity, it does tend to confuse any analysis of a World War One battle in which dominion troops were involved. By 1918, the troops supplied by the dominions had acquired a justifiable and enviable record as fighting formations for a number of reasons mostly unrelated to their origins. A number of British divisions had acquired similar reputations. In 1916, this was not the case. But it is also irrelevant.

This distinction between British and Australian appears to be of much greater concern to writers of today than it was to the troops in 1916. While there is evidence in the soldiers' letters home of a sense of difference between 'colonial' troops and soldiers from the British Isles, it can be argued that today's commentators have misinterpreted that distinction. The only clearly evidenced instance where the difference was substantial was in matters of discipline, where British involvement was vigorously opposed by most members of the Australian Imperial Force (AIF) with the exception of the senior Australian generals. Clearly some rivalry existed, but this was more likely to resemble that of the supporters of rival football teams. While most Australians of the AIF were proud of their national origin, they were equally proud to be British. In their letters home, many describe going to Britain on leave as 'going home'.

The bodies of three Australian soldiers killed in the portion of the German 2nd line which was held throughout the night by the 5th Australian Division during the Battle of Fleurbaix (as Fromelles was called in the early post-war years) which was fought on 19 and 20 July 1916. AWM A01565

# Casualty Figures

Casualty figures are a complex subject. While official figures can and usually do provide an accurate summary of the human cost of a battle, they should still be treated with caution. There are some critical rules and assumptions underlying both the way these figures are collected and what they mean. During World War One, when a soldier was killed on the battlefield and his body found, he was listed as 'killed in action'. If he was wounded and evacuated by the medical system, he was described as 'wounded in action'. If he died of that wound within a year of its being inflicted, he was recorded as 'died of wounds'. However, if he was only lightly wounded, or wounded but chose to stay with his unit, his wound may not even have been recorded. The real problems arose, however, with men classified as 'missing'. In the aftermath of a battle, the unit commander only gained an appreciation of the human cost to his unit when a roll call was conducted. The commander was then responsible for convening a formal Court of Inquiry which attempted to determine the fate of those lost. This was a legal process. The AIF administrative system advised the commander of those soldiers known to have been evacuated wounded or whose bodies had been recovered. For those who were classed as 'missing', the Court of Inquiry would attempt, by piecing together the available information, to decide what fate had befallen these men. Soldiers went missing in battle for many reasons: most were killed or wounded and their bodies never recovered. Others were captured by the enemy, thereby becoming prisoners of war, and their fate was not known for many months or years. Some were literally blown apart on the battlefield and no trace ever found. There are other problems with the statistics, however, and these often concerned the problems of definition. If a soldier was wounded and died more than a year after his wound, he was not counted in the statistics of that battle. This was of particular importance for gassed soldiers, who often lingered for years. The statistics do not discriminate between severe wounding and light wounds, nor do they record multiple wounding in the same action. Some soldiers were wounded and subsequently killed during the evacuation process. They could then be recorded as either killed in action or, if the final cause of their death was unobserved, recorded as 'died of wounds'. The potential for incorrect accounting increased if the soldier was wounded and captured by the enemy. The determination as to whether he was killed in action or died of wounds was not a priority for enemy soldiers collecting the dead and wounded and reporting is known to have been inconsistent. While in captivity, a soldier could have succumbed to wounds as a result of poor treatment or he could have died of sickness caused by inadequate medical attention. Finally, of course, for a very small percentage, 'missing in action' was the official accounting for someone who had deserted and managed to avoid detection. In a very few instances, deserters who had been reported killed in action were located years after the war had ended. Casualty figures should be used with great care and caution in arguments about the cost of a battle.

Apart from calls from some Australian politicians and some senior AIF officers, it is difficult to find convincing evidence that the creation of an identifiably separate Australian Army was desperately sought by the bulk of the AIF. Many even resented the 'Australianisation' of the senior command ranks of the Australian Corps in May 1918 which saw the transfer of several extremely popular British officers. The average digger seemed more concerned with remaining with his mates in a specific battalion. For today's commentators to discern something uniquely 'Australian' in the attitudes of the AIF on the battlefield requires a very narrow use of the available evidence.

The problem with much of the current debate over the history of the Great War is that it seeks to build the reputation of one or two groups by denigrating the efforts of others. Neither the Australians nor the Canadians need to have their fighting reputations enhanced by invidious comparisons with some less fortunate equivalent British formation. It is not necessary — the Australian digger was a brave, resourceful soldier who, by the end of that great conflict, was as competent and professional as any other on the battlefield.

No book on the Battle of Fromelles, especially one aimed at an Australian audience, can avoid the emotional dimension arising from the heavy casualty bill. The battle's status in Australia's military history is now firmly entrenched and, due almost entirely to the number of dead, still generates calls for greater formal recognition, including its addition as a battle honour for the battalions involved. While this emotional response is understandable, it does make dispassionate analysis of the battle difficult. Unfortunately for military historians of the Great War, there seems locked in the popular mind an unshakeable bond between the casualty count and the conduct of the battle. If the casualty count is high, then the battle was unnecessary, poorly planned and implemented, or futile. No amount of comparison with the casualty rates on D-Day, of Bomber Command losses in the next war or even the casualty rates in the victorious last months of the Great War can shake this connection.

This book does not attempt a detailed examination of all the nuances, aspects and issues that determined the course and outcome of the battle. Nor does it share the focus of most accounts on the men involved. It is intentionally more concerned with the command processes that led up to the battle and with the command and control of the battle itself. It is deliberately brief and has two separate purposes.

First, this book is intended to serve as an overview of the battle, with an emphasis on the strategic and military setting, a position from which this battle is so frequently removed. The second and more difficult objective is to persuade the reader to look beyond the standard explanations that 'it was the fault of incompetent, uncaring or obsessed British commanders' and understand that war is a dangerous, bloody business in which soldiers — sometimes lots of soldiers — die.

This book will also address some of the questions that underpin much of the popular criticism of the battle. Was it necessary? Was it poorly planned or poorly executed? Was it someone's fault?' Was the loss of so many men futile? There is not the space in a book of this type to analyse these questions in the depth necessary to resolve them. The book's intent is to provide a different way of looking at the battle, from outside the prism of the casualty count, and attempt to rehabilitate, if only a little, the reputation of those whose unfortunate responsibility it was to plan and conduct the attack.

France. c. 1918. A carrier pigeon being released from a British Army tank gun turret to carry information back to the pigeon base to be subsequently passed on to army troops. AWM H09572

# CHAPTER ONE

# PRELUDE TO A DISASTER

Within the vast body of writing that describes the Western Front, the greatest proportion is concerned only with small sections of a series of defensive works that ran from the North Sea to the Swiss border, a distance of approximately 750 kilometres. The Western Front presented a military problem without precedent. This defensive line had no flanks that could be turned without violating Swiss neutrality. Mobile warfare, which was the core tactical and operational skill of the armies of both sides before the war and the focus of their training, doctrine and equipment choice, was rendered irrelevant. The extraordinary numbers of troops assembled on either side of the trench-line — approximately 5,000 per 1.5 kilometres — allowed the front to be heavily garrisoned and substantial reserves to be retained for transfer to threatened areas.

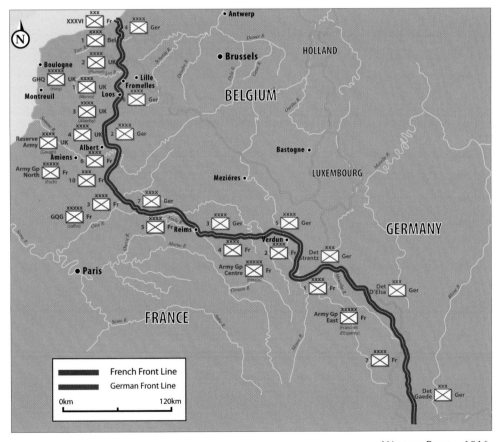

Western Front – 1916.
(Mark Wahlert)

# The Trench

Along with the grave headstone, the trench has become the defining symbol of the Great War. Unlike the headstone, however, 'trench' is an imperfect word to describe a complex and evolving defensive system. Trenches came in all shapes and sizes to suit a broad variety of purposes. There were saps, communication trenches, first line, second line and reserve line trenches, breastworks, covered trenches, jumping-off trenches, bunkers, pill boxes and observation points (OPs), to mention just the more common types. Trenches were just one part of the defensive system which included belts of barbed wire and other obstacles, interlocking machine-gun arcs and pre-ranged artillery. Trenches even acquired their own mythology, which holds that the Germans only built deep, secure and comfortable trenches supported by concrete bunkers and deep dugouts, while the Allied soldiers were forbidden to construct strong, complex defences for fear they would become too comfortable and refuse to leave them to attack the enemy. Neither story is true, although the Germans certainly led the way in developing trench systems, particularly in their innovative use of concrete and steel-reinforced strong points. Single lines of trenches were quickly replaced with multiple rows connected by deep communication trenches with embedded strong points for machine-guns, sniper positions and OPs. Pill boxes — the slang term for a concrete fighting position — and concrete shelters grew in number, design and complexity. Pill boxes were characterised by forward-looking apertures which allowed the occupants to engage the enemy to their front, while shelters presented a solid front and sides to the enemy and provided the occupants maximum protection from shellfire. The essential difference was that the occupants of the pill box could fight while remaining inside; the troops in shelters, however, had to leave their protection to fight. Trenches evolved as the growing power of artillery and new technologies such as the flame-thrower and the tank negated their protective advantage. By the end of the war, the best protection lay in leaving the formal trench defensive system and seeking cover in the mass of shell holes in No Man's Land because, if the enemy gunners knew the position of a trench, they could destroy it.

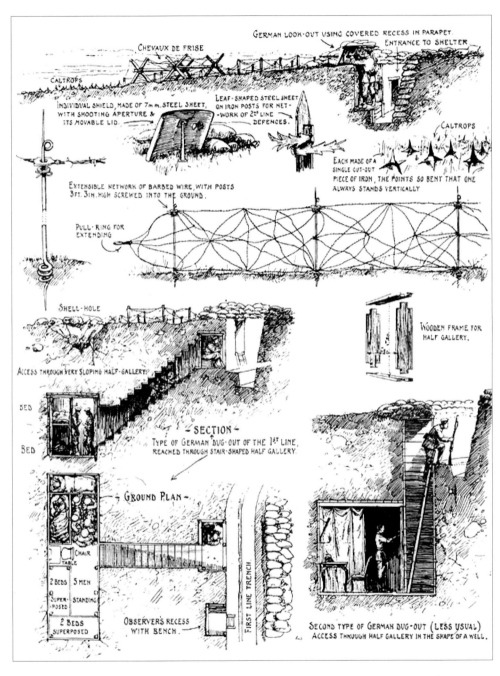

World War One Trench Diagram.
(Australian Army Training Pamphlet)

15

The origins of the Battle of Fromelles can be traced to the beginning of the war and the failure of the German strategy for a quick victory. Despite the French victory at the Battle of the Marne (5–10 September 1914) which halted the German advance, and the end of the so-called 'race to the sea' when both sides attempted outflanking manoeuvres that ended at the coast of the North Sea, the Germans retained the strategic advantage. They occupied over a quarter of France, including some of the most resource-rich and industrialised areas, and over 90% of Belgium. Securing a German victory was merely a matter of holding this territory until the Allies, lacking the will or the resources necessary to drive them out, were compelled to seek a negotiated peace settlement. To a certain extent, this strategy was forced on the Germans by their situation in the east. Their Austro-Hungarian allies had proven militarily fragile and required German troop support to avoid being knocked out of the war. By adopting a defensive posture in the west, Germany was able to send significant numbers of troops east in support of its allies. Not surprisingly, it was the Germans who fully developed and exploited the trench as the predominant defensive structure in this war.

With the Germans occupying much of France and most of Belgium, it was politically impossible for the Allied High Commands to 'do nothing'. Had they fought a defensive war on the Western Front and negotiated a solution — as so many critics later suggested they should — they would have been dismissed. From the moment the BEF arrived in France, British General Headquarters (GHQ) was under constant and intense pressure from its French equivalent, GQG, to take the offensive. France, in particular, had recent experience of negotiated peace with Germany and the domestic French political temper was clearly unwilling to swallow another dose. Nor should there be any doubt that the Germans would have extracted a heavy price for a negotiated settlement. The Treaty of Brest-Litovsk is irrefutable proof of Germany's capacity to drive a very hard bargain. There is no indication that the Germans planned an early withdrawal from the occupied territories — indeed the evidence suggests the reverse, as they took the trouble to rename all

## The Treaty of Brest-Litovsk

The Treaty of Brest-Litovsk was the peace treaty Germany signed with the new Bolshevik government of Russia on 3 March 1918 that ended Russia's participation in World War One. The treaty demanded huge territorial and material reparations from Russia on a scale not demanded even by the vilified Versailles Treaty that ended the war. The Germans demanded one quarter of Russia's population, one quarter of its industry and 90% of Russia's coal mines. The Russians had to pay six billion German marks in war reparations.

the French towns, villages and roads in the occupied sector. Fromelles, for example, was renamed Petzstadt.

Germany's strategic advantage enabled it to remain on the defensive and force the Allies into launching expensive frontal attacks on well-prepared and well-sited positions. Having captured so much Allied territory, the Germans were able to cede some less defensible areas and retreat to the most defensible terrain. The Allies were forced to do the bulk of the attacking, on ground of the defender's choosing and frequently uphill. The attacker was almost always disadvantaged in this static war, particularly given the difficulty of securing operational and tactical surprise. The Germans' ability to select terrain to maximise their advantage was a major tactical, operational and strategic edge that is rarely acknowledged by critics of the conduct of the war.

Photo taken during the excavation phase demonstrating the dominating position of the Fromelles church.
(Australian Army photo)

The political ability to surrender territory and retreat to the best defensive terrain, thereby determining where future battles would occur, was not an option open to Allied commanders. This gave the Germans unprecedented advantages in securing tactically important ground such as heights or areas protected by rivers or heavily wooded terrain. Fromelles is a clear example of a battle in which the advantage of terrain lay heavily with the German (in this case Bavarian) defenders. Fromelles sits on a feature known as Aubers Ridge. As Peter Pedersen notes: 'Actually to call it a ridge is to abuse the word. Stretching northeast from La Bassée for twenty miles to 17 the west of Lille and nowhere more than 120 feet above sea level, it is more like a flattened speed bump on the ironing board flat plain that rolls north to Armentières.' Nonetheless, the ability to observe Allied movements for kilometres behind the lines was to be a major advantage in the coming battle and reflected the ongoing German defensive edge that contributed heavily to the bloody fighting that was to precede the final victory in 1918.

A view from the high ground: Fromelles, France, 11 November 1918. AWM E04032

# CHAPTER TWO
# THE STRATEGIC SETTING

Given the sheer scale of the Great War, particularly on the Western and Eastern Fronts, the reasonable reaction of many historians has been to treat their subject of interest in isolation from its context for ease of explanation and analysis. Yet this approach does not always serve the subject well. Events taken out of context can be misconstrued, as key influences may be overlooked or accorded less weight in their explanation. The best known example of this is the debate over the infamous British operation in Flanders in 1917, known to history as the Battle of Passchendaele. The decision to mount this operation only makes sense when considered against the backdrop of the submarine campaign against Britain, the state of the French Army, the situation in both Russia and Italy, and Britain's long-term strategic imperatives on the Continent. The same rationale applies to the Battle of Fromelles. Valid analysis is only possible if the action is considered in the context of the surrounding strategic, operational and tactical circumstances.

Despite popular opinion, few commanders in armies of modern democratic nations are incompetent dolts incapable of planning a battle or unconcerned about casualties. Unquestionably they make mistakes and one consequence is that soldiers are killed. Context is a determining factor in understanding the decisions of any commander. Armies are used by their governments for political ends — and armies are not lightly sent to war. The commanders of those armies are expected to win the war — and wars are not won by commanders who are afraid to suffer casualties in their own army. A general who does nothing to bring an end to a war will enjoy a short tenure; indeed World War One is replete with examples of generals sacked by their Kaiser, government or high command for not demonstrating a sufficiently aggressive approach to victory. All commanders of higher level formations plan operations that will materially aid the attainment of victory in as short a time as possible. This is the general overarching strategic context against which all actions and all commanders of the Great War should be considered.

## Progress of the War

By 1916, the war had settled into a relatively predictable pattern. On the Western Front, once their initial invasion of 1914 had been halted, the Germans adopted a largely defensive strategy. Throughout 1915, the French (and increasingly the British) mounted offensives aimed at driving the Germans back, albeit to no avail. On the Eastern Front, the sheer size of the battlefield still provided opportunities for manoeuvre warfare. However, Russia discovered that a mass army is not, in itself, sufficient to guarantee victory. From the outbreak of the war, Russia's ability to mount sustained attacks and retain captured ground was severely hampered by poor leadership, the lack of an industrial infrastructure and flawed logistical support. As 1915 wore on, the Germans gained the ascendency over the Russians and Russian victories were increasingly won against the Austro-Hungarian Army rather than the Germans. Of real benefit to Britain and France, however, was the impact of the Eastern Front in continually distracting the German High Command. The constant demands from the east for troops and materiel ensured that the Western Allies never had to face the might of the German Army in its entirety.

On the periphery of the war, other political and military events also served to distract both sides. Turkey and Italy entered the war, producing other lines of conflict that diverted troops from the main theatre. In Britain, political opinion concerning the possibility of attacking Germany in areas other than northern France and Belgium created conflict and confusion with opinion divided as to where the main emphasis should lie. Politically inspired, unsuccessful 'side-shows' such as Gallipoli and Salonika served to distract the Allied military effort. Italy proved to be of questionable military value as her army was even less prepared for the conduct of modern warfare than that of her principal foe, Austria-Hungary. Both Britain and France were forced to send troops later in the war to prevent the Italian Army's total disintegration.

While 1916 was no more a 'turning point' in the course of the war than any of the other years, it was undoubtedly a significant year as it featured three of the defining battles: Verdun, the Somme and, on the Eastern Front, the Brusilov Offensive. This year also saw the first real attempt by the Allies to coordinate their operations and the appearance of major new technological innovations on the battlefield. Of the three major battles, two were the result of the Allied strategy to launch attacks on several

### 1916- A Turning Point?

Several notable British military historians challenge this view, arguing that 1916 was the year the British Army began its steep learning curve on the tactics and technologies required to achieve victory.

fronts simultaneously — an attempt to combat the German ability to transfer troops rapidly between fronts to meet single attacks. The other, Verdun, pre-empted the Franco–British assault and resulted from a German plan to destroy the French Army. These battles arose from the recognition that the war could only be resolved by the destruction of the enemy's capacity to continue fighting: that is, by the destruction of his armies. While appalling in its conception, attrition warfare was the only real tactical option available to either side to win the war in 1916. No general, including General Haig, the man most maligned for employing this tactic, set out to casually destroy his army or his soldiers. Conversely, it was the failure of alternative strategies that forced attrition warfare on commanders for whom seeking a negotiated peace was simply not an option. As had already become clear to both sides, the science of the defence held the ascendency over the science of the attack. This ascendancy would persist until 1918 when tactical and technological developments gave the Germans a brief offensive ascendency in the early part of the year and Allied scientific and military development coincided with a fundamental collapse in German industry and society from July. Thus the circumstances required for an Allied victory were created.

A photograph taken of Field Marshal Sir Douglas Haig on Armistice Day 1918. Haig is in the centre of the front row. To his left is Sir Henry Rawlinson with General Plumer to his right. Between Haig and Rawlinson, in the second front row, is General Sir William Birdwood.
AWM H12241.

In 1916, both sides were still confronting a strategic situation for which neither had planned, neither was equipped to deal with, and neither possessed the tactical, operational and strategic skills to overcome. The strategic military setting prior to Fromelles was shaped by the challenges facing all the combatant nations as each tried to adapt political and economic systems to the demands of industrialised warfare. Each nation's logistics system struggled not only to deliver the vast quantities of ammunition and materiel necessary for this form of warfare, but also to source supplies. National industrial capability, even in France and Germany, was totally unprepared for the level of demand of all manner of military materiel, from ammunition to wood for trenching. The Germans held the advantage initially in terms of war production, but their failure to achieve a quick military victory eventually exposed their weak strategic, political and economic position.

## War on Two Fronts

The Germans were fighting a war on two fronts. In the west they faced an industrial power and, to the east, they confronted a nation whose manpower resources had exercised a mesmerising effect on German planners for decades. The German planners had good reason to be concerned for, in 1914, the Russians boasted a standing army of 1,423,000 and could call on a further 3,115,000 with the outbreak of the war. Another 2,000,000 reservists could be mobilised within three months.

### France versus Germany: basic comparison

| INDICATOR | GERMANY | FRANCE |
|---|---|---|
| Population | 68 million | 39 million |
| Coal production | 191,500,00 metric tons | 41,000,000 metric tons |
| Lignite production | 87,500,000 metric tons | None |
| Steel production | 17,000,000 tons | 5,000,000 tons |
| Railway track | 61,000 track kilometres | 49,500 track kilometres |

*Source:* Robert Doughty, *Pyrrhic Victory: French Strategy and Operations in the Great War,* Belknap, Cambridge Massachusetts, 2005, p. 115.

The two Western continental powers (France and Germany), with their established and well-exercised conscription systems, did not share the same pain of expansion experienced by the British Army. Yet they still faced the problem of balancing the needs of the army against the requirements of the industries supplying that army. France, handicapped by its smaller population, was forced to call up many of its skilled workers in 1914. Despite the recognition that without them French industry was struggling to cope with the demands of war production, the French Army only very reluctantly and belatedly allowed some of its skilled workers to return to the factories. All sides turned increasingly, and successfully, to women to fill the manufacturing labour shortfall.

This 1919 photograph illustrates clearly the growth in size and sophistication of British shells during the war. As well as having to learn the basic science of shell production, British industry had to develop, test and prove entirely new types of shells. It is a major but unrecognised British achievement that, within the four short years of war, an entirely new, massive and sophisticated shell manufacturing and filling industry was created.
AWM E05483

The famous British shell shortage of 1915 was replaced by the equally famous shell unreliability problem of 1916, when an estimated one third of all field artillery shells fired either failed to explode or exploded prematurely. For their part, the French had experienced similar problems even earlier in the war. In struggling to build production capacity, industry (both British and American) initially cut corners on quality and safety, to the detriment of both its workers and the troops using its munitions.

While the poor quality of British shells provoked a scandal, the British had few options available to remedy this. The only alternative at the time was to limit the supply of shells to the front while industry developed the necessary skills in both manufacturing and quality control. This 'solution' would have been equally unacceptable to the army. This problem was not new and remains an issue to this day. Modern societies do not maintain capabilities such as artillery shell production 'just in case', so a production lag in building such capabilities is inevitable unless governments and taxpayers are prepared to fund the continued existence of unnecessary production capacity through the many years of peace.

More so than the other major powers, Britain also had to change its national mindset before its army could become totally effective. For centuries, British strategy had remained focused on avoiding continental entanglements, sheltering behind the protection of the world's strongest navy and using its financial strength to engage others to fight its wars. By the early twentieth century, Britain's focus was fixed firmly on its empire, not on Europe. In the ninety-nine years between the battles of Waterloo and Mons, the British

## British Army Evolves

The British Army was taking tentative steps towards developing the types of structures and skills required to fight a continental war. In response to its failings in the South African War, the British had established an Imperial General Staff by 1909 and organised a Territorial Force of reservists to support the standing army. Unfortunately for the British, these essential innovations were still in their infancy at the outbreak of World War One.

Army fought seventeen major wars around the world, most of which were small-scale and often fought using Indian or colonial troops. The British Army was not designed to fight a continental war and British society was not conditioned for the potential economic demands and heavy human costs of warfare on the continental scale. The British government delayed implementing many essential domestic political measures in response to the needs of the war. Arguably it was not until Prime Minister H. H. Asquith was replaced by David Lloyd George on 7 December 1916 that the British government finally became totally committed to the war effort. The same year saw the British turn to American bankers to fund the war, thus mortgaging Britain's financial future and sowing the seeds of her eventual decline as a world superpower.

Prime Minister David Lloyd George. AWM H16845

One significant military example of this confused national priority lay in the failure of the War Office and the India Office to cooperate on the employment of the Indian Army forces. The Indian Army represented the single largest standing military force in the Empire; yet it was never fully committed to the war in Europe. It was inevitable that this political indecision and confusion would affect both the command process and the supply system in Europe. Nor was this merely a civilian or political problem. The military senior officer 'trade union', with the notable exception of Sir Douglas Haig, vigorously resisted the appointment by Lloyd George of the civilian former head of the North Eastern Railway, Sir Eric Geddes, as head of the military transport system in France and Belgium. Ultimately, Geddes' appointment dramatically improved the supply and transport support for the BEF. The industrial changes and parallel societal upheavals caused major problems for the military in 1915 and 1916 through the inability of the nation to satisfy even basic materiel requirements such as guns, shells and vehicles.

Despite this national confusion and political opposition, by 1 July 1916, Great Britain had assembled the largest military force ever deployed by the British Empire. In addition to maintaining the world's largest navy as insurance against military disaster on the Continent and, while creating thousands of new war factories with additional demands for skilled manpower, Britain was still able to expand the BEF to over 1.5 million men by 1 July. The British government had finally introduced conscription in early 1916, almost two years after the outbreak of the war. These political and economic achievements were still overwhelmed, however, by the massive military problems confronting the Allies in 1916.

## Military Technology Issues of 1916

In August 1914 all the protagonists anticipated a short, sharp war of manoeuvre. While this was the tactical and operational characteristic of the opening and closing months of the war, the almost three-and-a-half years of the middle period were typified by static warfare in fortress-like conditions with no scope for sweeping outflanking manoeuvres. The Germans, whose pre-war planning aimed to provide a military solution to the problem posed by the ring of hostile fortresses on her western border, began the war far better equipped with heavy artillery. Neither side, however, possessed the wealth of specialised equipment or specific training that trench warfare would demand. Basic infantry equipment such as machine-guns and hand grenades were comparatively rare (less so for the Germans) and their use was poorly understood. The French began the war in highly visible, colourful uniforms, a political legacy rather than a sop to military conservatism. The bulk of the available artillery — light field guns — fired mainly shrapnel ammunition. This was highly effective against troops in the open but largely ineffective against men sheltering in trenches and dugouts. The effect of trench warfare was to force a return, at least on the Western Front and at Gallipoli and Salonika, to military tactics resonant of earlier, siege warfare ages. Trenches and concrete strong points became the new castles while mortars and howitzers were the modern equivalent of the trebuchet. The year 1915 was characterised by the attempts of both sides to come to terms with this new 'old' way of waging war.

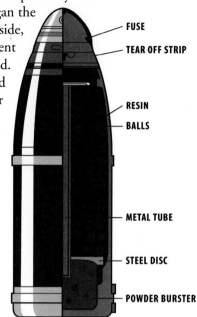

FUSE

TEAR OFF STRIP

RESIN

BALLS

METAL TUBE

STEEL DISC

POWDER BURSTER

Cross section of a shrapnel shell. (Mark Wahlert)

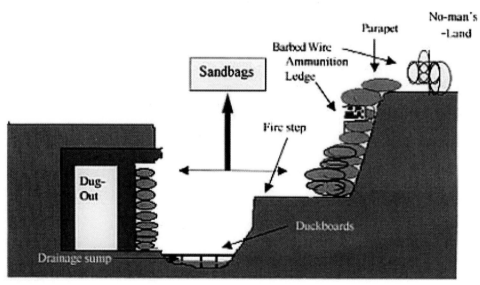

No-man's -Land

Parapet

Barbed Wire
Ammunition
Ledge

Sandbags

Fire step

Dug-Out

Duckboards

Drainage sump

Simple diagram of a typical early trench.

(Source of illustration unknown)

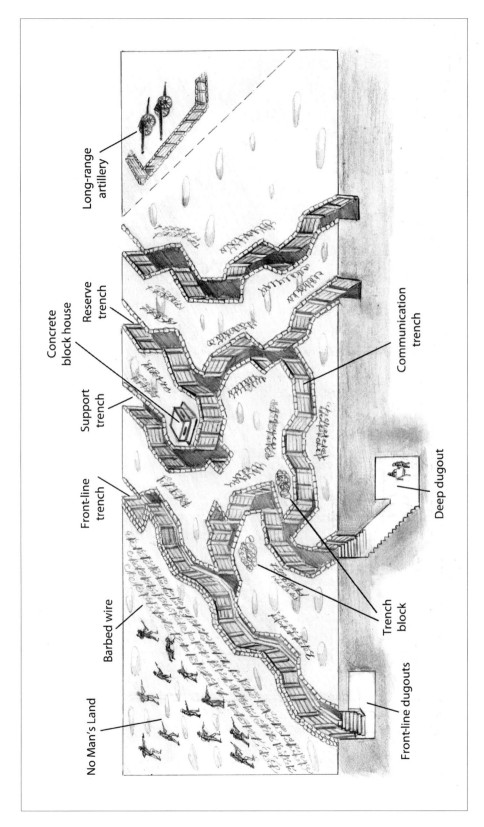

Trench system. (Jeff Isaacs)

# Big Bertha

| | |
|---|---|
| **Calibre:** | 420mm (16.53in) |
| **Weight:** | 43 tonnes |
| **Length:** | 5.88m |
| **Crew**: | 200 |
| **Effective Range**: | 14km |
| **Manufacturer:** | Krupp Corporation |

In 1908 Gustav Krupp built a gun for the German Army that was capable of destroying the heaviest fortification. This massive weapon could fire an 820 kg shell over 10 kilometres. Although the name was commonly applied to a whole variety of large-calibre German artillery guns, 'Big Bertha' (*Dicke Berta*) actually referred to a single siege gun, at that time the world's largest and most powerful. Up to twelve Big Bertha-type howitzers were produced, the first two just after the onset of hostilities in 1914. With a range of 14 kilometres, their 420mm shells proved devastating and four were used during the German assault on Verdun in February 1916.

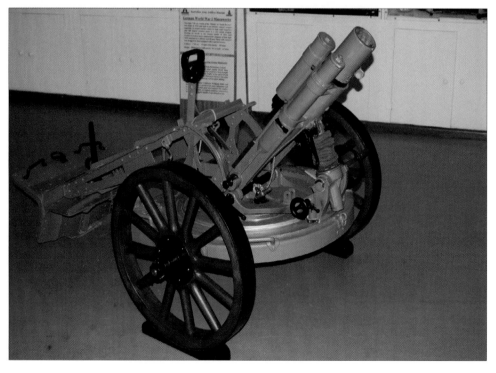

German light *minenwerfer* fully restored and on display at the Australian Army Artillery Museum, North Fort, Sydney.
(Photo Major John Gallagher, Australian Army Artillery Museum)

One solution vigorously pursued during 1915 was a search for weapons more appropriate to this new military problem. Machine-guns and hand grenades proliferated. New weapons, such as trench mortars, were devised to deal with the problem of hard-to-hit fortified positions and deep, narrow trenches. The Germans, as the leading European producer of advanced chemicals before the war, retained the advantage in developing completely new types of weapons. They were the first to develop and use poisonous gas on the battlefield, an initiative which gave the Allies an immense moral and propaganda advantage. They were also the first to employ flame-throwers. Older technology was developed further while innovation emerged at an unprecedented rate. Guns became bigger and more plentiful, barbed wire thicker and more difficult to cut and, eventually, new armoured vehicles with trench-crossing capability arrived to return some form of mobility to the battlefield. Medical skills developed rapidly, ensuring that, for the first time in warfare, more deaths were caused by battle than by sickness. These medical developments were not achieved solely for humanitarian reasons; they were essential to minimise the decline in combat power that resulted from reduced manpower. The ability to heal a wounded soldier and return him to the front line was a major force multiplier.

Gas mask. (Jeff Isaacs)

## Gas

Allied propaganda scored major successes in the neutral world by depicting the Germans as capable of any atrocity. In fact, ultimately, the British became the experts in the use of gas on the Western Front and as many Germans were to die from this weapon as did Allied soldiers.

# The Artillery

Before the outbreak of war, British artillery was divided into two formal groupings. The Mounted Branch consisted of the Royal Horse Artillery, supporting cavalry divisions, and the Royal Field Artillery which supported infantry divisions. The Dismounted Branch comprised the Royal Garrison Artillery which provided heavy and siege artillery support for the army in the field. While experiences in both the Boer War and the Russo–Japanese War had highlighted the need for heavy artillery support, most of Britain's first line artillery was light and intended for mobile warfare. Field artillery operated closely with the division it was supporting, often located in the front line alongside the infantry. The gunners fired at targets they could see — referred to as 'direct fire'. While effective when engaged in manoeuvre warfare, direct fire was rapidly rendered ineffective by the static nature of the war on the Western Front. Targets were obscured and the guns themselves were rarely exposed in the front line. 'Indirect shooting', a technique formerly more the preserve of the Garrison Artillery, now had to be mastered by all branches. This technique involved the gunners firing on targets they could not see, their fire adjusted by observers with visibility of the target. The observers adjusted the range and direction of the fire by watching where ranging shots fired by the guns fell and shortening or lengthening the range and moving the direction left or right until the ranging shot hit the target. The observer would then confirm that the guns were on target and the planned artillery program could begin. It was (and remains) a complex skill.

Central to the new technique was communication. The observer had to call adjustments to the batteries clearly and quickly. In this war, the gunners developed and jealously guarded a telephone network (known then and now as a 'net') independent of the normal command network so that the vital adjustment of fire was not interrupted or delayed by other messages. However, communication with the front line was often tenuous, so other more primitive means were used, such as coloured rockets and flares that had a predetermined meaning depending on the composition and sequence of the various colours. For this reason, the gunners were also quick to embrace the new technology of the wireless and, by the end of the war, were regular users.

The other technology that radically altered the gunners' technique was the aeroplane. While small artillery observation parties could operate in or even forward of the front trench-line, gunner observers on the ground could not see targets or ranging shots that landed well behind the enemy lines, in dead ground or from the reverse slopes of hills. This was a major handicap to the heavy artillery which looked to exploit its range and fire deep into the enemy's rear areas. Despite this handicap, long-range guns could and regularly did fire on specific features such as crossroads or rail terminals, bridges and other 'choke points', features which could be identified from maps and from which the term 'map shooting' was derived. However, as the fall of shot could not be observed from the ground, the value of the long-range artillery was much reduced. Observers mounted in aircraft could spot and adjust the fall of shot from even the biggest and longest ranged guns and, for this reason, artillery spotting became one of the principal operations undertaken by aircraft during the war. Airborne observers could see the full extent of the battlefield and locate all potential targets and, unlike observers on the ground, could track the progress of their attacking infantry. Much of the airborne reconnaissance was conducted to assist the planning of artillery actions.

Perhaps most importantly, the critical deficiencies in tactics and arsenals were exposed by the series of bloody but inconclusive battles fought in 1914 and 1915. British artillery was outnumbered, outweighed and out-ranged by its German counterpart. French artillery included more heavy artillery, although most of this was obsolete. The French fascination with 'morale' and 'the spirit of the offensive' saw many French infantry killed in ill-advised, poorly prepared frontal attacks on well dug-in German positions. Recognition of the reality of the new type of war soon saw major changes in basic French tactics, although it was no easy matter to overturn ingrained military tactics in a short time. The importance of learning from experiences on the battlefield was accepted by both sides and there was a flourishing industry in capturing, translating and circulating among the troops 'lessons learned' material from the other side.

Both sides also recognised the importance of aircraft, particularly their employment for tasks such as reconnaissance and artillery spotting. The technological race to dominate a new battlefield had begun. Air power was both a technology and a concept. In addition to acquiring new types and greater numbers of aircraft, both sides had to learn how to develop and exploit the capability this new technology offered. The presence of aircraft also forced major changes in all aspects of the military art. The aircraft's ability to penetrate far behind the lines meant arcane military specialties such as camouflage, deception, concealment and dispersal of assets, now became vitally important. New capabilities, such as anti-aircraft artillery, had to be developed. With the arrival of the aircraft, achieving operational and tactical surprise on the battlefield became immeasurably more difficult. The Allies could generally boast air superiority over the Western Front battlefields of 1916, but the Germans managed to achieve air control over critical sectors for specific periods, especially later in the Somme operation. The High Command on both sides clearly understood the contribution of air power to the course of the battle, which undermines the popular view of the generals as technophobes grimly clinging to tradition.

## The Military Situation in 1916

The Battle of Fromelles began on the night of 19 July 1916 and ended early the next morning. It involved an attacking force of two divisions pitted against one German (Bavarian) division. In the context of the Western Front, this was a small action. As argued earlier, it is important to place Fromelles in the context of the war in 1916. A brief outline of the other actions of early 1916 is thus necessary to allow the outcome and consequences of the Battle of Fromelles to be judged against those of other battles that year. This will enable the reader to determine whether these were simply the phenomena of that particular war, or evidence that the outcome of Fromelles was due entirely to the actions of the commanders on the ground.

The year 1916 was characterised by big battles. For the Allies, these battles were born of the realisation that, through concerted, coordinated attacks, they could prevent the Germans shuttling troops around to face individual attacks or to reinforce threatened fronts. This recognition and the plan to capitalise on it in 1916 emerged during the Chantilly Conference at which the four Allied powers — France, Great Britain, Russia and Italy — agreed to launch a coordinated series of attacks in the spring. These assaults were to be launched primarily against the German armies, with the Russians to attack on the Eastern Front, the British and French on the Western Front and the Italians resuming their Isonzo Offensive against the Austro-Hungarians. Their focus was the destruction of the German Army in the field.

The German Army had also been planning. Its *de facto* Commander-in-Chief, General Erich von Falkenhayn (see biographical notes), was determined to destroy the French Army. He had identified the British Empire as the principal enemy, but also recognised that, protected by the Royal Navy, Great Britain was a difficult land power target to destroy. Falkenhayn advised the Kaiser that British strength, both industrial and military, was growing and that immediate action was vital. His plan was to attack Britain and eliminate her through the destruction of one of her allies — ideally the French. (It was a similar strategic assessment that led Britain into the Gallipoli campaign, with similar outcomes.) Falkenhayn described the French Army as the 'sword' of Britain and deduced that its destruction in 1916 would force the British out of the war. He also recognised the risks to his own army inherent in costly frontal assaults, and was determined to destroy the French indirectly, primarily through the use of artillery. Ironically, the use of artillery, rather than infantry, to achieve the intended outcome was also the original concept for the Battle of Fromelles.

# Aircraft Manufacturing Company (Airco) DH. 2

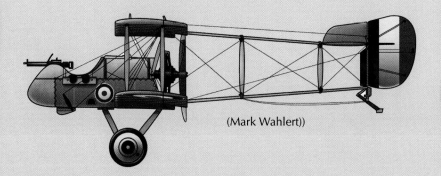

(Mark Wahlert))

| | |
|---|---|
| **Type:** | Scouting 'pusher' biplane |
| **Wingspan:** | 8.61m |
| **Length**: | 7.68m |
| **Powerplant**: | One 100hp (75kW) Gnome Monosoupape rotary engine |
| **Max Speed**: | 150kph |
| **Armament**: | One forward-firing .303in (7.62mm) Lewis gun |
| **Ceiling**: | 1300m |
| **Range**: | 400km |
| **Endurance**: | 2hrs 45mins |
| **Crew**: | One |

The second dedicated fighter squadron to deploy to France in World War One was No. 24 Squadron, Royal Flying Corps (RFC), equipped with the new Airco DH. 2. The DH. 2 was a single-seat 'pusher' type whose prototype had been trialled successfully in France in 1915 and deployed operationally in early 1916. The 'pusher' concept was important to the RFC as its nemesis, the Fokker *Eindecker*, had a synchronised, forward-firing machine-gun, a development that had eluded the British. Nevertheless, the DH. 2 proved a successful design and enabled the RFC to counter the 'Fokker scourge' that had given the Germans the advantage in the air war since late 1915. During the Somme Offensive in July and August 1916, No. 24 Squadron destroyed thirty-eight Fokkers. Their dominance over the Somme was short-lived, however. By September 1916, with the arrival of the new German *Halberstadt* D. II and *Albatros* D. I, the DH. 2 was outclassed. It was progressively replaced during 1917 by more capable British fighters.

# Fokker E. III (*Eindecker*)

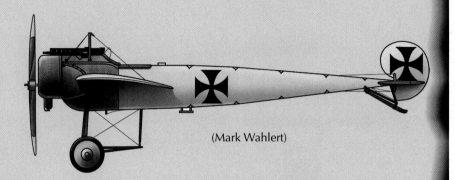

(Mark Wahlert)

| | |
|---|---|
| **Type**: | Fighter |
| **Wingspan**: | 9.52m |
| **Length**: | 7.3m |
| **Powerplant**: | One Oberursel U. I 1 Rotary Engine, 99hp (74kW) |
| **Max Speed**: | 150kph |
| **Armament**: | One 7.92mm (.312in) Parabellum MG14 machine-gun |
| **Ceiling**: | 3600m |
| **Range**: | 198km |
| **Crew**: | One |

The Fokker *Eindecker* (Monoplane) was a German single-seat monoplane aircraft, the first purpose-built German fighter and the first aircraft to be fitted with synchroniser gear enabling the pilot to fire a machine-gun through the arc of the propeller without striking the blades. While of a basic design and unremarkable in performance characteristics, its revolutionary gun allowed the German Air Service a degree of air superiority from July 1915 until early 1916. This period was known as the 'Fokker scourge', during which Allied aviators regarded their poorly armed aircraft as 'Fokker fodder'. The deployment in early 1916 of the new British Airco DH. 2 and Royal Aircraft Factory F.E. 2 'pusher aircraft', along with the French *Nieuport* 11, brought the dominance of the *Eindecker* to an end. The two most famous *Eindecker* pilots were Oswald Boelcke and Max Immelmann.

# Verdun

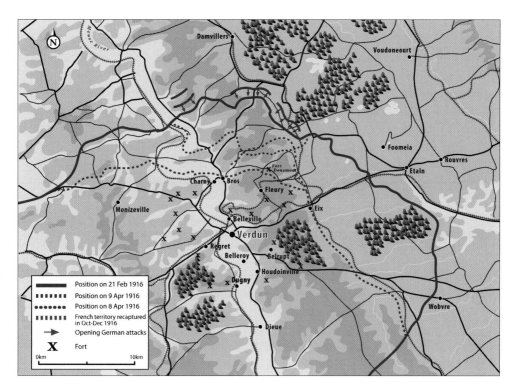

Verdun.
(Mark Wahlert)

Falkenhayn's plan was subtle yet complex. He looked for an objective which the French would never surrender and against which he could concentrate his artillery. Then, he reasoned, by merely threatening to capture the objective, the French Army would march into his artillery trap and be destroyed. At one point Falkenhayn claimed he did not even need to capture Verdun to cripple France — just killing French soldiers would suffice. Clearly, it was not just the maligned British generals who understood that killing large numbers of enemy soldiers was a major strategic option for winning the war.

Falkenhayn found the ideal location for his attack in the historically significant fortress complex centred on Verdun, astride the River Meuse. The German general recognised that Verdun was culturally and politically such an important symbol of France that the French would use all their military resources to protect it. The German plan was to seize the hills to the east of the Meuse, forcing the French into a series of deadly frontal assaults to recapture them.

Prior to the attack, the Germans amassed over 1,000 heavy guns on a front of just over twelve kilometres — one gun every twelve metres. To sustain his artillery, Falkenhayn had amassed a stockpile of over two million shells (unlike British shells in 1916, German shells actually worked). The standard light and medium artillery was tasked with destroying the French defences and defenders while the heavy artillery was carefully positioned to interdict the French supply and reinforcement lines. Falkenhayn acknowledged that he had insufficient troops to undertake a full-scale attack on both sides of the Meuse and planned to attack on the eastern side only. Given his initial strategy of drawing in the French, the plan appeared sound, but later, as the strategy unravelled, this was to have serious consequences for the Germans. Despite his manpower problems, Falkenhayn still managed to allocate ten divisions — about 150,000 troops — to the attack. Secrecy was paramount and, for the first time in history, aircraft were used to prevent the enemy conducting reconnaissance operations over the German forces' assembly area.

The French Commander-in-Chief, Marshal Joffre, had anticipated an attack at Verdun but assumed that it would not begin until April. As he could see no possible strategic benefit for the Germans in capturing the city, Joffre considered the action to be a diversion. He was wrong on both counts. Against the better judgements of a number of French commanders, the defences at Verdun had been allowed to deteriorate. French strategists had questioned the defensive value of fortresses in view of the German destruction of similar defences at the beginning of the war. As a result, much of the artillery had been removed to support other threatened areas of the line. When the attack began, the French had only 270 guns to support the defenders, many of which were obsolete. There had been little maintenance or improvement to the defences around the forts and, in some areas, defensive fortifications consisted simply of ditches. Barbed wire was in short supply and the garrisons had been seriously reduced. Very belatedly, the French High Command began to redress the problem, but shortages of men and materiel meant little improvement had been made before the attack began. Fortunately for the French, two additional divisions were despatched to Verdun just in time.

Falkenhayn initiated his plan, 'Operation Judgement', on 21 February 1916 after a week's delay due to atrocious weather. This delay allowed the two new French divisions to integrate into the defences in time to meet the attack. Initially, Falkenhayn's plan worked reasonably well, although inevitably not as well as anticipated. After a nine-hour bombardment, the heaviest of the war to date, the Germans advanced some eight kilometres, occupying much of the targeted high ground east of the river and, as a bonus, capturing the dominating Fort

Douamont and other forts along the way. While the Germans were surprised, much like the British some months later, by the number of defenders who had survived the opening bombardment, they suffered only localised delays (although the many tales of heroic resistance do tend to obscure this unpalatable fact). The Germans' use of mobile flame-throwers on the battlefield at Verdun introduced yet another frightful aspect to trench warfare.

The image shows an obsolete French 155mm gun being prepared for action by Italian soldiers in 1918. Being obsolete did not mean that the gun was useless on the battlefield, but it was hardly a match for the modern weapons of the age.
AWM H05108

The French reaction to the German assault has been the subject of much controversy. While they eventually moved to defend both banks of the River Meuse and Verdun itself, it is clear that, at the time, Joffre was prepared to abandon both. Only the snap decision by his Chief of Staff, General de Castelnau, to send forward the French reserve, General Philippe Pétain's Second Army, saved the French from the loss of Verdun. Now the plans of both sides began to unravel. The German command, encouraged by its success and 'the offensive spirit' of the fighting troops, abandoned the idea of merely threatening Verdun and moved to capture it. The French were gripped with determination to resist at all costs. The initial German strategy was vindicated by the French reaction, but their abandonment of this strategy led to a bloody stalemate which proved as costly for them as for the French.

Falkenhayn's decision to attack on only one bank of the Meuse left the French artillery on the other side free to exact a heavy price on the attacking troops. The narrow focus of the German attack also made it vulnerable to artillery from several directions, although it was the French artillery on the left bank of the Meuse that eventually halted the German attack. Once the German momentum was lost, the battle settled into the familiar attritional slogging match.

While Verdun had cost the French dearly in both losses and in the confidence of their troops, the Germans had also been denied the victory they sought. With almost the same number of casualties sustained as were inflicted on the French, with no significant advances or new resources captured, Verdun was clearly a German strategic failure. The excuse to abandon the battle was provided by the impending British attack on the Somme — ironic perhaps, as the ultimate aim of Verdun was to end the war before the British could build a serious military capability to be used against the Germans.

## The operational lessons of Verdun

There are inherent dangers in launching an attack before all levels of command clearly understand the objectives, the methods to be used and the resources available. Changing the overall plan once a battle has begun introduces significant risks and a high potential for failure. Verdun demonstrated the very real need to shape the battle to the available resources. Ambitious objectives with inadequate resources cost both sides dearly.

The consequences of Verdun were felt as far afield as the Eastern Front where the Russians were preparing to launch their offensive as part of the Chantilly strategy of coordinated attacks. Given the enormous pressure on the French, the impending Russian offensive had a secondary objective of diverting German troops from Verdun to meet the eastern threat.

# Flame-Thrower

Lieutenant Leslie Bowman Cadell, 6th Battalion, holding
a German Flammenwerfer (flame-thrower) captured
near Stirling Castle in the Ypres sector during September
1917. AWM Image E00802

The German *flammenwerfer* was used during World War One primarily to clear trenches and bunkers. A devastating weapon when used at close range, it was often just as deadly for the operator as the fuel in the flame-thrower could be ignited by a bullet strike or explosion. In addition, *flammenwerfer* crews were shown little mercy when captured. Germany introduced two flame-throwers early in the war. The first, the smaller and lighter version known as the *kleinflammenwerfer*, was designed to be carried by one man and crewed by two. Using pressurised air and carbon dioxide or nitrogen, it belched forth a stream of burning oil to a range of 18 metres. The second, the *grossflammenwerfer,* was a larger and heavier device which had a maximum range of almost 40 metres but required a team of up to six men to operate. While initially used against French troops in October 1914, the flame-thrower earned its terrifying reputation when employed in a surprise attack on the British at Hooge in Flanders in July 1915. In two days of severe fighting the British lost thirty-one officers and 751 other ranks. Given the success of this attack, the Germans promoted widespread use of the device across all fronts of battle.

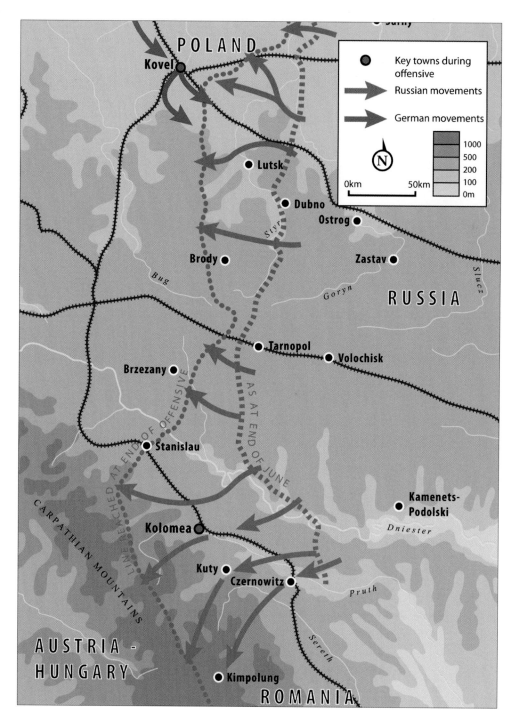

Brusilov Offensive.
(Mark Wahlert)

# The Brusilov Offensive

Not all the Russian Army commanders supported the idea of a major offensive. Many had been severely mauled by German operations in 1915 and believed the Russian Army needed time to rebuild and re-equip. The Russian front line was broken into three separate commands termed 'fronts' and, of these, the commanders of the north-western and western fronts were unconvinced by the strategic arguments in favour of a combined offensive. Only the commander of the south-western front, General Alexei Brusilov (see biographical notes), favoured the planned coordinated attack. Perhaps unfortunately for the overall success of the strategic plan, General Brusilov's command faced the Austro-Hungarians rather than the Germans who were the intended target. In the face of such divided opinion, the Russian High Command eventually agreed that Brusilov would attack first with the others to assault later. This agreement would prove costly for Brusilov who would be given no additional resources. However, his decision to proceed with the offensive was further justified by the need to rescue the Italians from a major Austro-Hungarian advance on the Isonzo that threatened to knock Italy out of the war.

Brusilov's aim was to capture Kovel, an important Austro-Hungarian rail centre in the north, and Kolomea in the south. However, the principal purpose of his plan was the destruction of the Austro–Hungarian Army, thus forcing both reinforcement by the Germans from the Western Front and the movement of Austro-Hungarians from the Italian Front. To achieve this ambitious aim, Brusilov organised his army group of forty infantry divisions and fifteen cavalry divisions into four separate armies.

Brusilov planned to attack on a broad front, using all his forces with no reserves. This meant an attack on a 300-kilometre front by 200,000 men supported by 900 guns. Recognising the risks involved in a broad frontal assault, particularly without overwhelming numbers, Brusilov shrouded his attack in secrecy, effectively concealing his build-up. He also planned the use of new tactics, with small groups of infantry employed in a 'shock' role that hinted at the German 'storm troop' tactics of the following years (this supports the contention that this tactical innovation was not solely a German idea). In another tactic foreshadowing developments later in the war, he planned a short, intensive bombardment rather than the drawn-out preparatory barrage common at the time. His use of these short bombardments to maintain tactical surprise was mimicked in the 'hurricane' barrages developed by both sides on the Western Front in 1917 and 1918. To minimise exposure to defensive fire, his troops dug jumping-off trenches within metres of the Austro–Hungarian line. Preparations for the attack were reputedly the best ever undertaken by the Russian Army during the war.

The Russians faced a combined German and Austro-Hungarian force of five armies totalling over 150,000 men and 600 guns. They occupied well-prepared positions and their morale was boosted by their recent victory against a Russian attack at Lake Naroch in early March.

Brusilov attacked on 4 June, his emphasis on achieving tactical surprise paying immediate dividends. After a week's intensive fighting, the Russians on the northern and southern parts of the line had advanced over fifteen kilometres. The Austrian *7th Army* was verging on collapse and was eventually split in two. With this success, some additional troops were made available to maintain the Russian momentum. Brusilov now insisted that the attack could only continue if the commander of the Russian Western (or Central) Front, General Alexei Evert, immediately launched his own new offensive. Eventually Evert launched his offensive, but only after a lengthy delay and with little success.

After a brief pause in July, Brusilov launched two more attacks which saw the Russians advance over 160 kilometres in the south and reach the Carpathian Mountains. The advance was less successful in the north and central sectors and finally ran out of steam on 20 September 1916.

While its initial success appeared to justify Brusilov's plan, the reality was that the plan was fatally flawed. With all his troops engaged, Brusilov lacked the ability to exploit important successes, maintain his lines of communication and extend his supply lines as the advance continued. He was unable to secure his flanks adequately — a situation exploited by the counter-attacking Germans, especially on the northern shoulder of the advance. The cost to both sides was enormous with estimates of between 500,000 and one million Russian casualties and one million to 1.5 million Austro-Hungarian. The Germans suffered around 350,000 casualties.

At the strategic level, Brusilov's offensive appears to have had some effect on the Western Front as significant German reinforcements were transferred to the eastern theatre. Brusilov effectively destroyed the Austro-Hungarian Army as an independent military force, as future operations were planned and directed from Berlin. His successes also contributed indirectly to the dismissal of Falkenhayn as German Commander-in-Chief and his replacement by Paul von Hindenburg.

## Operational Lessons of the Brusilov Offensive

An army that lacks certainty and confidence in its fighting ability is unlikely to achieve lasting success on the battlefield. If this lack of confidence is combined with the absence of a clear goal and defined limits to an attack, the potential to defend early gains on the battlefield is low. In Brusilov's case, the only apparent intention was the simple destruction of the Austro-Hungarian Army. This vague goal, combined with the lack of sufficient forces to exploit any successes achieved and with troops who lacked the confidence to act independently if local reverses were experienced, meant the attack did not have a natural 'end point'. Defenders were thus able to slow the advance, regroup and launch limited counter-attacks that caught the attackers disorganised, exhausted and beyond the range of their combat supply lines. This enabled the defenders to inflict unsustainable casualties on the attackers. By their very nature, vague, poorly planned attacks such as this rarely achieve significant long-term gains and frequently leave the attacker strategically and tactically worse off.

## The Somme

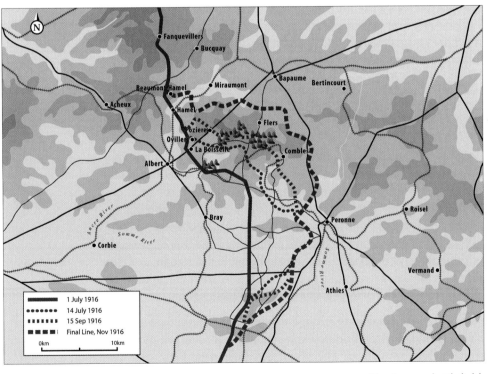

The Somme battlefield.
(Mark Wahlert)

The battle of 1916 most closely linked to Fromelles was the Battle of the Somme which raged intermittently from 1 July to 18 November. Arguably the most infamous and least understood military operation in the English-speaking world, the Battle of the Somme has been presented as an encapsulation of all that could go wrong in a military operation. The focus on huge casualties for small territorial gain has rendered it almost impossible for historians of the Somme campaign to change popular perceptions that the battle was a complete and unnecessary disaster. Certainly, the Somme is the battle that has come to define combat on the Western Front. Other battles, especially the successful, but still costly, advances in late 1918, are virtually unknown and almost discounted by the general public. Indeed, it is almost impossible to reconcile the popular view of warfare on the Western Front, as presented with depressing regularity in the popular media, with the awkward fact that ultimately the British and French armies prevailed. The casualties suffered, especially by the British, have also effectively obscured the reasons the battle was fought and any military successes, short or longer term, that were achieved. The casualty count, approximately 20,000 killed on the first day, has earned a place in history as the British Army's greatest disaster. Yet, as a percentage of those actually fighting, the casualty rate for the British Army in the Normandy campaign was higher. What is often overlooked is the fact that the casualties on the Somme were inflicted on the largest British Army ever fielded and thus came as a shock to a British public much better prepared for the casualty rates of a small army engaged in Imperial policing duties.

Contrary to popular belief, the Somme was not an ill-planned example of dull-witted generals sending troops to their death simply because their leaders were short of ideas. The planning process was characterised by months of staff work and the final orders filled hundreds of pages. Indeed, it could be, and has been, argued that the plan was too detailed, too inflexible and too prescriptive. While there is still much controversy about the details underpinning the decision by the British High Command to commence a major operation in July against the Germans on the Somme, it is now accepted that, due to French insistence, General Haig had little choice in either the timing or the location of the attack. The reason the battle was fought, and the priorities for the varying objectives set for the battle, were constantly changed during the planning and implementation phases.

Also contrary to popular opinion, the battle commander, Sir Douglas Haig (see biographical notes), was no dim-witted fossil out of touch with the realities of war. The obstacles confronting him when he assumed overall command in December 1915 were sufficiently overwhelming and complex to have destroyed a less resolute character.

He had been in overall command a mere six months when the battle began, and had inherited the Allied strategic plans for the year. This allowed him little time to learn his new job while simultaneously focusing on developing a sophisticated contribution to the agreed plan to defeat the Germans in 1916. His on-the-job training can only have been further complicated by the constant strident French demands for immediate action and rumbling political disquiet on the British home front. This is not to suggest that Haig did not make mistakes. Unfortunately, the mistakes he made, especially in setting unrealistic objectives, translated into heavy casualties.

## Kitchener's Army

'Kitchener's Army' was the popular term applied to the British equivalent of the AIF: the all-volunteer army raised by Great Britain between August 1914 and December 1915. The name originated with the man who was responsible for its creation — Secretary of State for War, Field Marshal Lord Kitchener. The raising of this force was a major success for Great Britain with 2,466,719 men enlisting during this period. Regrettably, even this mass of enthusiastic, committed volunteers was insufficient to maintain the British Army at the size necessary to engage in industrial age warfare against continental-sized enemies. While Kitchener's Army provided the vast bulk of the British commitment to Fromelles and on the Somme during 1916, Britain was ultimately forced to rely on a conscript-based army to win the war.

Haig faced two major challenges on assuming command of the BEF. He had to supervise the operational and detailed tactical planning for the first major Allied attack of the year which, unhappily, was also the first substantial British attack to rely on the untried troops of the 'Kitchener' wartime volunteer army. In addition, Haig had to oversee the expansion of his forces, coordinate support arrangements with the French, assess the strengths and weaknesses of his subordinate commanders and decide who would be given responsibility for the tactical conduct of the battle. In addition to a half-trained army, he was faced with a logistics support system still in chaos, an ammunition crisis and shortages of practically every type of military materiel. He was also aware of a looming manpower problem. The British government, forced to abandon the volunteer principle that had sustained the war effort so far, introduced conscription for single males in January 1916 and extended this to married men in April. While perhaps a side issue, Haig must also have questioned the loyalty of troops from Ireland and the potential of the Easter Uprising in Dublin to disrupt Irish recruiting.

Planning for the Battle of the Somme began almost as soon as the Chantilly Conference of December 1915 ended. Initially, the British High Command had favoured an offensive in Belgium early in 1916, a preference which was supported by the French Commander-in-Chief, Joffre, only if it was conducted as part of a series of operations intended to wear down the German defenders across the whole front. Joffre expected the British to mount other attacks in the early spring of 1916 as a preliminary to a major offensive that would deliver the *coup de grace* to the German Army. This French embellishment of the British concept caused considerable disquiet, mainly due to its apparent attritional focus and lack of Belgian support. The uncooperative attitude of the Belgians can only have assisted support for the Somme campaign. The Belgians were resolutely defensive, their Commander-in-Chief asserting their categorical preference that any offensive operations should occur on French rather than Belgian soil. On 14 February 1916, Haig (somewhat unwillingly) and Joffre had agreed to an amended plan for a combined offensive on the Somme to begin in July 1916. Seven days later, Falkenhayn launched the attack at Verdun. At this stage of the war, Haig was acutely aware that the British were the junior partner in the coalition, and so was less inclined to argue British concerns with his allies. He was deeply worried by the BEF's preparedness to undertake such a major operation although, as the early months of 1916 passed, this concern was overridden by the greater fear that the French Army would not survive the slaughter at Verdun.

The plan for the Somme operation had to evolve as the battle at Verdun ebbed and flowed, and thus it was forced to be dynamic and reactive. Originally, the French had taken the lead in both the planning and the provision of the major strike element for the offensive. But Verdun changed all this. Britain now assumed almost full responsibility for planning the battle. Verdun had cut the contribution the French could make to the offensive, although they still provided eleven divisions. Argument continues over the real purpose of the Somme operation. Those who seek to malign Haig, its commander and chief planner, assert that beneath the military-speak that obscured its real aim, the Somme was intended to be purely attritional. Others, including the Official Historians, argue that the battle was intended to be a strategic victory that would result in the defeat of the German Army and, shortly thereafter, the end of the war. Gary Sheffield, one of the most authoritative historians on the battle, has observed that the real aim of the Somme was a combination of both these intentions. Those supporting the strategic nature of the battle are inclined to argue that a combination of factors, including many beyond the control of Haig, caused the operation to fail to achieve its strategic goal.

Haig's critics lose sight of the fact that Haig was trying to win the war and that defensive strategies simply would not achieve this. Haig had initially shied away from a purely attritional battle as he was not convinced that this would result in a decisive outcome. However, the impact of Verdun on his French allies caused him to reassess his approach. He appears to have eventually planned a three-stage battle. The preliminary attack would see the assaulting troops make inroads into the enemy's defences; during the attrition stage the defenders would exhaust themselves trying to eject the attackers and prevent further advances; and in the final, or exploitation phase, the defending enemy would lose its ability to resist and be defeated. Unquestionably, Haig believed his attack would achieve a strategic victory. He was well aware that the Germans had suffered as much at Verdun as the French. British and French intelligence services, both before and during the battle, continually provided Haig with optimistic assessments claiming the fighting strength of the German defenders was declining as was their morale. Logic dictated that, if the French doubted their ability to hold on much longer, then the Germans would likewise be unable to maintain the rate of additional loss inflicted on them by the onset of a major British offensive.

The commander appointed by Haig to oversee the tactical battle, Sir Henry Rawlinson, was less convinced of this outcome. This was to be an early round of the continuing debate between those generals who favoured smaller, but achievable, objectives and those who sought objectives that, while a remote possibility, would end the war. Henry Rawlinson was an early supporter of the 'bite and hold' strategy in which objectives set for the battle were modest but attainable. 'Bite and hold' meant capturing a small section of the enemy's line, consolidating it and building up for another attack before repeating the cycle. It was a slow and methodical answer to the problems of trench warfare which enabled the attacker to move forward and seize ground. This approach did not, however, offer the prospect of a crushing strategic victory or a result that would end the war. Consequently, it held little appeal for Haig, who was convinced that the circumstances were ripe for a major victory. No rational commander could ignore the prospect of a strategic victory. Despite tactical misgivings prompted by reports of failure to cut the wire or sections of enemy trench remaining intact, the attack went ahead on 1 July 1916.

Sir Henry Rawlinson in his advanced headquarters during the Somme campaign. AWM E03898

As with Fromelles further north, the Somme battlefield is defined by the presence of higher ground, in this case the chalk ridge running from Thiepval in the west to Morval in the east. The Germans held this high ground and had established a formidable defensive line characterised by a combination of fortified villages and strong points on the forward slopes which provided the outer crust of the defensive system. Supporting elements, such as artillery, supply dumps and formation headquarters, were located in the dead ground behind the ridge, out of sight of ground-based artillery observers in the British lines. The broken nature of the terrain, with spurs and gullies within and behind this outer line, further strengthened the defences by providing oblique lines of sight for machine-guns and hidden positions for trench mortars. Many of the natural characteristics of the Somme also rendered it a particularly tough proposition. The chalk rock was soft enough to cut but sufficiently resilient to withstand shellfire from all but the heaviest guns. This enabled the Germans to dig deep, complex, shell-proof shelters and turn the villages in the forward zone into fortresses with strong points and underground communication trenches.

# Bite and Hold Tactics

'Bite and hold' tactics were the tactical manifestation of the military problem facing both sides during this war. From the moment the war of manoeuvre was halted by the trench system that snaked its way across Western Europe until the advent of the sophisticated weapons systems of 1918 (based on tanks, mobile artillery, aircraft and fluid, flexible infantry tactics), the trench system gave the defender an almost unbeatable advantage. Put simply, an attacker could usually occupy the front lines of the defender's trench system. He could, if the attack was sufficiently well planned and resourced, penetrate to the second or even (as happened at Arras in 1917) the enemy's third line of defences. What no attacker could do prior to 1918 was exploit this penetration and achieve a breakout behind the enemy defence lines. There were a number of reasons for this. The defender brought his reserves, supplies and artillery forward to the battle across established and well-developed lines of communication on a broad front. The attacker had to feed his follow-on forces — his forces of exploitation — through a narrow gap in the enemy's defences across broken ground with no roads or railways and, in some places, in conditions impassable even to horsed traffic. It was impossible to move the essential supporting artillery forward fast enough, and with sufficient ammunition, to cover the exploiting infantry. Commanders on both sides had long recognised this problem. For the Allied commanders — under political pressure to make tangible progress which was measured in terms of recaptured ground — simply awaiting a technical solution was not an option. A compromise approach was developed whereby attacks were limited to tactical, rather than strategic success. The method followed was to set objectives that required the capture of limited lengths and depths of the enemy's front line. Such objectives could be achieved, as they involved successive steps that allowed artillery to be moved forward at each step to prepare for and protect the next attack. New troops could be brought into battle comparatively slowly and ammunition levels maintained. The only problem with this method was that, given that it was slow and methodical, it allowed the enemy to develop new defensive lines to counter any progress. 'Bite and hold' operations provided the Allies with limited successes, allowing the relentless forward grind of the Allied armies and the recovery of small parts of occupied territory, but 'bite and hold' was never going to win the war.

The German defensive strength was not unappreciated by the British. The attack was preceded by the largest British artillery barrage of the war to that date. A total of 1,010 field guns and light howitzers and 427 'heavies', together with another 100 French guns, battered the German front lines in front of the British positions for seven days, firing prodigious amounts of ammunition. Unfortunately, the massive bombardment did not achieve its aim. Artillery is a complex science and many of Haig's gunners were inexperienced or poorly trained, and failed to hit their targets. Many rounds dropped short, killing their own troops, while failing to suppress the German artillery. As many as one in three of the shells fired failed to explode which, given that over the course of the battle the British fired some 19 million shells, represented a serious setback. As a consequence, the attacking infantry frequently found their path blocked by uncut barbed wire obstacles and German trenches and strong points that remained intact. German artillery freely engaged the attacking infantry as they crossed the exposed ground. By contrast, further south, eighty-four batteries of French heavy artillery obliterated the opposing German guns and much of the German field defences opposite General Fayolle's Sixth Army, enabling the French to make significant advances on the first day.

France c. 1916. British Army railway-mounted heavy gun in action. AWM H08474

At 7.30 am on 1 July 1916, over 100,000 British troops left the shelter of their trenches and attacked a 27,000-metre section of the German front line, from Serre in the north to Montauban in the south. Three French corps attacked the Germans north and south of the Somme River. The first day's objective was to capture the German front line positions as far as Pozieres in the north and Montauban itself in the south. The objective for the second day was the German second line defences while, by day three, the British were to have punched a hole in the German defences sufficiently large to enable the exploitation forces, including three cavalry divisions in the Reserve Army, to move behind the German defenders and roll up their flanks. On the British southern flank, the French were to drive through in support. Unfortunately, while incurring over 60,000 casualties including 20,000 killed, the British forces failed to achieve any of these objectives. With the effective support of the French, the British attack in the south made the best inroads but, in most sectors, the front line barely moved. The Somme operation, on which so many hopes for a quick end to the war rested, quickly settled into a Verdun-like dour bloody struggle. Progress was made, but at a terrible cost.

A British Mark 1 tank – this one is a 'male' type armed with 6-pdr cannon. AWM H19323.

The struggle on the Somme — not one continuous battle but rather a series of sequential and linked attacks and periods of consolidation — continued until 18 November 1916. Subsequent attacks often employed new tactics and technologies as the troops of both sides learned new skills and refined current techniques. New technologies, notably the tank, and new techniques, including the tactic of small groups of infantry moving independently of one another, helped improve tactical effectiveness, although none offered the prospect of winning the war on its own. It would be another two years before the refinement of an effective combined arms tactical doctrine, technological improvements in the tank, communication systems, aircraft and artillery provided the Allies with complex capable weapons systems that could defeat the German Army in the field.

It is not the purpose of this book to examine the Battle of the Somme in any depth. Importantly, however, the Somme was both the cause and the backdrop for the Battle of Fromelles. The opening assaults on the Somme occurred over the first three days of July. The huge losses and the minute gains achieved forced a pause in the general attack, while plans and resources were prepared for a resumption of the general attack, known as Phase Two, on 14 July. However, in the period from 3 to 13 July, there was little respite for many of the troops. Fourth Army launched a further forty-six local actions, often poorly prepared and inadequately supported, aimed at preparing the positions for the resumption of the offensive. The objective for this second phase, agreed at a meeting with Joffre on 3 July, was the German second position between Longueval and Bazentin le Petit. Rawlinson and the commander of XIII Corps, Sir Walter Congreve, devised a plan 'that was daringly different from that of 1 July'. The attack would be launched at dawn, with only a brief but intensive barrage to prepare the position, the troops forming up during the night of 13-14 July. Haig was concerned that the poorly trained troops would become confused and that they would not be ready for the dawn advance, but in the end he agreed to Rawlinson's plan. The troops formed up in the dark in No Man's Land and advanced close behind the barrage, which allowed them to move into the enemy trenches before the Germans emerged from their shelters. The attack was a great success.

The follow-on exploitation was less successful, however, and eventually the advance stalled in fierce fighting for Delville and High Woods. The success of the opening phase is easily explained. Rawlinson used approximately 66% of the number of guns used on the first day of the Somme to 'soften up' just over 5% of the ground shelled that day on the Somme. With more than three times as many shells targeting the enemy's defences, the problems of uncut wire and surviving enemy strong points that so disastrously slowed the attackers on the first day of the battle were largely overcome for this attack. Other lessons were learned but the one with most relevance to Fromelles was that adequate artillery preparation was essential for the success of an infantry attack. Unfortunately, with fewer than five days before the launch of the Fromelles attack, there was no artillery reserve available to move north to provide additional support.

Following the early success and subsequent disappointment of the second phase, the British High Command relied on Fourth Army operations to renew the advance. Having demonstrated its ability to gain ground, the High Command was infused with the sense that a similar success could be achieved. While Fromelles was viewed as a diversion and a 'fixing operation', the operations by the 9th Division (including the South African Brigade) to clear Delville Wood were regarded as central to the resumption of the offensive. The advances of the French Army south of the Somme River added to this sense of anticipation. It is hardly surprising in such an atmosphere that the operation of just two divisions well north of the 'main game' should not receive the same degree of command attention and support as the Somme sector.

## Operational Lessons of the Somme

The lessons from the Somme filled innumerable British Army pamphlets and exercised the minds of many military analysts during and after the war. The most important lesson was that commanders should only set objectives that their force is capable of achieving. In the context of the Somme, a second and related lesson was always to be wary of overly optimistic intelligence estimates of the enemy. Proceeding with an operation despite critical problems in one's own forces, on the basis of intelligence advice that the enemy is in a worse position, is a high risk strategy. The basic lesson that inadequate artillery preparation of an objective, especially a hardened strong point, makes it almost impossible for an infantry attack to succeed was relearned almost daily. The Somme also proved that, in industrial-scale warfare, it is the number of effective shells fired, not the skills of soldiers, which will decide the outcome.

# CHAPTER THREE
# THE OPPOSING ARMIES

## Britain and the Empire's Forces in 1916

Despite the impression created in some popular histories, Australia did not win the war on its own and nor did Great Britain. On both sides, this was a coalition war and the role and contribution of each partner varied considerably. From the start of the war in August 1914 until July 1916, the French and Russian armies did most of the fighting for the Allies. Indeed, given the British military performance during August and September 1914, the French held legitimate concerns over the willingness of the British to fight at all. The Russians also complained about the perceived reluctance of both Western allies to remain on the offensive with the onset of trench warfare in 1915. From July 1916, however, the involvement of British Empire forces increased incrementally until, by the end of the war, the British played a major part in the final defeat of Germany. The reason for this pattern of involvement lay in the markedly different levels of preparedness of the coalition partners as they entered the war.

### Comparative Strengths of the Opposing Armies

| Nation/ Empire | Population 1914 | Peacetime Strength end July 1914* | Mobilisation Strength end August 1914 | Strength at end of war | Notes: * full-time regulars, not part-time |
|---|---|---|---|---|---|
| Australia | 4,872,000 | 2,989 | 65,000* | 298,000# | * includes 45,000 militia for home defence # 185,000 overseas |
| Austria-Hungary | 49,900,000 | 450,000 | 3,350,000* | 2,229,500 | * 2,000,000 sent to the front |
| Belgium | 7,517,000 | 47,000 | 177,000* | 145,000 | * 35% fortress troops |
| France | 39,600,000 | 739,000 | 3,781,000 | 2,794,000* | * 2,562,000 on Western Front |
| Germany | 67,000,000 | 880,000 | 4,500,000 | 4,200,000* | * 3,400,000 on Western Front |
| Russia | 167,000,000 | 1,423,000 | 5,000,000* | Defeated | * only 40% fit for front-line service |
| Serbia | 5,000,000 | 30,000 | 460,000 | 110,500 | |
| United Kingdom | 46,400,000 | 247,500 | 733,500 | 3,196,000* | 1,561,00 on Western Front |
| United States | 92,000,000 | - | - | 1,982,000* | On Western Front |

*Source:* John Ellis and Richard Cox, *The World War 1 Databook: The Essential Facts and Figures for all the Combatants,* Aurum Press, London, 1993, p. 245.

When Britain declared war on Germany on 4 August 1914, its empire was woefully unprepared for a war on the scale required. The British Army totalled only 247,000 regulars, of whom over a third were based in India or other overseas stations. This was essentially a small professional army tailored specifically for Imperial police duties. The British Army was not designed to fight a war on the Continent against the mass, conscript-based armies of the major European powers. It lacked the numbers, the equipment and the tactics to operate in such an environment. Of consequence for Fromelles, its commanders had no experience in handling troops in formations larger than a corps, and even corps-level manoeuvre was a very recent experience for British senior officers. The British Staff System was a recent innovation, adopted reluctantly as a consequence of the Esher Report which detailed the fiasco of the Boer War.

The newly constituted BEF comprised six hastily assembled infantry divisions and one cavalry division. Four of the infantry divisions and the cavalry division were sent to France in August following the declaration of war. The deployable military strength of the entire British Empire numbered just over 125,000, with the whole British pre-war army comprising only eleven divisions — about the same number as tiny Serbia. Most of these troops were scattered across the Empire, often in battalion-sized groups. One commentator described the British Army initially despatched to France as 'so small as to be but a drop in the ocean of armed men hurrying to confront one another on the plains of Belgium.' By July 1916, when the Battle of Fromelles was fought, the British Empire's military forces in France and Belgium had expanded ten-fold to over 1.5 million men. The expansion in equipment and materiel was even more marked and continued to accelerate for the remainder of the war as British and American war industries increased production.

**Growth in British Artillery Strength.**

| Date | Field Guns and Light Howitzers | Heavy Guns and Heavy Howitzers |
|---|---|---|
| August 1914 | 462 | 24 |
| June 1918 | 5,482 | 1,227 |

# Size, Organisation and Composition

For readers new to military history, the size, organisation and composition of the various units and formations encountered can be extremely confusing. To some extent the military, particularly the British military, makes understanding this basic information unnecessarily complex by using the same name for different types of units. For example, a brigade of infantry is quite a different formation from an artillery brigade. A British regiment is entirely different from an American or Continental regiment. In 1916 the smallest grouping of infantry soldiers was the section, consisting usually of about fourteen men. Four sections together constituted a platoon. The platoon, of around sixty men, was theoretically commanded by a lieutenant or second lieutenant, although casualties in this category of officer were so high that platoons were more often commanded by sergeants. The platoon was the smallest grouping of soldiers commanded by a commissioned officer. Four platoons comprised a company, normally commanded by a major or a captain, with a strength of about 240. Four companies plus a headquarters company made up the battalion — the basic building-block of the infantry. With an authorised strength of around 1,032 (but rarely up to full strength) and commanded by a lieutenant colonel, the battalion was the 'home' for the infantry of the AIF. Initially four but, following the 1917 reorganisation, three battalions together formed the next grouping, the brigade. Commanded by a brigadier general, the brigade was the first level of organisation in which the commander would be a remote figure to the troops under his command. With a normal strength of around 4,000, the brigade was also the first level at which permanent specialist troops were included in the formation. At brigade level, this included machine-gun companies and light trench mortar companies. Above the brigade was the division. If the battalion was the infantry building-block, the division was the building-block of combat power for the army. Divisions were self-contained fighting formations, including for the first time other combat and combat support elements alongside the infantry. There were artillery brigades, engineers, signallers, pioneers and medical and veterinary units. Divisions had their own transport elements, including specialist ammunition supply units known as columns. A division, commanded by a major general, usually numbered around 18,000 soldiers. The next organisational grouping was the corps — a particularly flexible structure. Commanded by a lieutenant general, the corps could consist of just one or two divisions or as many as five or even six. Corps were assembled for specific purposes and changed constantly, with divisions moving between corps on a regular basis. The only exceptions were the 'colonial' corps formed late in the war. Both the Canadian and Australian Corps benefitted from some stability in command when they were formed in late 1917-early 1918, as all the national divisions were permanently assigned to their national corps. Corps included many specialist troops such as heavy or siege artillery and aviation forces assigned to divisions in support of specific operations. The second highest organisational grouping, as fluid in its size as the corps, was the army, commanded by a general. Early in 1916, Britain fielded four armies on the Western Front, each nominally consisting of four corps. However, the number of corps assigned could and did vary, depending on the operation the army was tasked to undertake. On the first day of the Battle of the Somme, for example, Fourth Army comprised five corps. The highest formation was the BEF, the term covering all British forces on the Western Front. The BEF was commanded by a field marshal.

Britain only just survived the destruction of its small but highly professional pre-war army in 1914 and the devastation of its trained reserve forces in the bloody battles of 1915. By 1916, the volunteer forces known as 'Kitchener's Army' and the early conscript forces had become the major components of the new BEF. One serious effect of the savage casualty rate in the first two years was the loss of the potential new group of leaders, both officers and non-commissioned officers (NCOs), for this new, amateur army. The experienced privates who would have been the sergeants of the expanded army were lost learning the skills critical to those who would come later. On a smaller scale, but of greater impact for the successful prosecution of the war, was the loss of trained staff officers and middle rank officers who would have been the planners and commanders of this new force. Infantry privates and lieutenants can be trained relatively quickly. Training someone to command a division or plan a battle takes years.

### British Empire General Officers (including Brigadier Generals) Killed, Wounded, Missing or Prisoners of War

| Year | 1914 | 1915 | 1916 | 1917 | 1918 |
|------|------|------|------|------|------|
|      | 10   | 47   | 48   | 51   | 76   |

*Source:* Frank Davies and Graham Maddocks, *Bloody Red Tabs: General Officer Casualties of the Great War 1914-1918*, Leo Cooper, London, 1995, p. xii.

Britain had been slow to adopt the continental General Staff System (another consequence of its Imperial policing focus) and, when war broke out, many of its carefully trained staff officers were killed fighting with their regiments. The lack of trained instructors and the constant demand for replacements forced the British to cut their traditional training syllabus to focus on the basic skills for the conduct of trench warfare. The loss of other battle skills, especially the ability to conduct fighting retreats and manoeuvre, was to become an issue in 1918, when the German Army launched its final mass offensive, shattering the strictures and predictability of trench warfare. But no-one could have foreseen this in 1916.

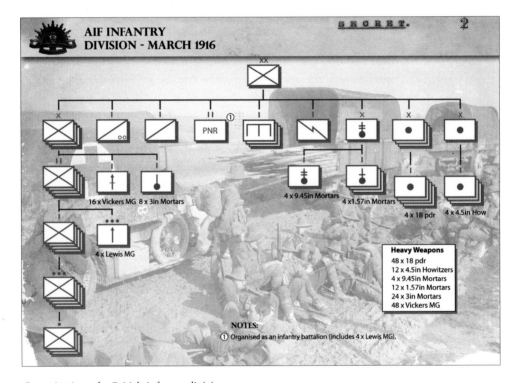

Organisation of a British infantry division.
An explanation of the symbols used in this and subsequent diagrams appears at the end of the book. (Mark Wahlert)

Between January and July 1916, the BEF grew from a combat strength (that is, combat soldiers only, excluding combat support and logistics personnel) of 450,000 to over 660,000, organised into four armies. The strength of individual armies varied, depending on their future role. For example, the attack on the Somme was to be mounted primarily by Fourth Army which, by 1 July, had increased in size to over 400,000 combat soldiers. The primary combat formation was the division — on the Western Front, this was the infantry division. The approved strength of a division changed throughout the war as technology gradually replaced manpower and replacements failed to keep pace with losses. In 1916, the combat power of the standard division lay in its three infantry brigades, each of around 4,000 soldiers, and its artillery brigades of another 3,000. Other divisional troops, including transport, medical and engineering elements, increased the standard 1916 division to an official strength of approximately 18,500 men. Divisions were rarely at full strength, their numbers depleted by casualties, troops away on leave and on courses, and troop detachments to form short-term work parties for corps or army tasks. Organisational changes also had a major impact on divisional strength. The artillery went through several major overhauls with more and more guns grouped into corps and army-controlled units. On the other hand, numbers frequently increased, particularly if a division was preparing for an attack. Additional artillery support was available, either under command or on request. Extra engineer and pioneer support could be provided also to help consolidate captured enemy positions and build communication trenches in newly captured ground.

At the other end of the BEF pyramid, the infantry tactical assault elements of the army, change was also rife. The composition of an infantry assault team altered as infantry experience grew and new tactics and technologies evolved. In 1914, infantry tactics centred on the rifle and bayonet, with companies and half-companies providing the tactical manoeuvre element. The basic combat grouping was the half-company, comprising one officer and fifty-five soldiers, grouped into two rifle sections of twenty-seven men and a small headquarters section. By late 1916, platoons and specialist sections had replaced the half-company as the basic manoeuvre element. The platoon, now the smallest officer-led grouping on the battlefield, comprised four specialist sections. The most important was the light machine-gun section with a Lewis gun, the gunner, his No. 2 and eight dedicated ammunition carriers. There were two sections dedicated to the new weapon of trench warfare, the grenade.

# Grenades

The outbreak of World War One found the British well behind the Germans in the development of the grenade. As early as August 1914, the Germans had a stockpile of 70,000 hand grenades and a further 106,000 rifle grenades. By the time of the Battle of Fromelles, grenades, employed by specialist soldiers known as grenadiers, had become as important in trench warfare as the bayonet. With the development of the grenade and innovation in its use, bombing parties grew in size and frequency. By late 1916 an Australian bombing team usually comprised up to ten men: an NCO, two throwers, two carriers, two men with bayonets to defend the team and three 'spare' men to replace casualties. As a raiding party progressed down a trench-line, the grenadiers (or bombers in the AIF), would throw grenades into each dugout they passed, or use grenades to clear a path ahead of the team. Probably the largest grenade battle of the war occurred near Pozieres on the night of 26-27 July 1916. For more than twelve hours, the Australians and Germans exchanged grenade fire until a combination of casualties, exhaustion and a depleted stock of grenades brought the exchange to an end. The Australians threw some 15,000 Mills Bombs during the night; the Germans, using various types of grenades, expended a similar quantity. The Mills Bomb was the outstanding grenade of the First (and probably the Second) World War. Despite the variety of grenades brought to the field by the Germans, the ingenuity in their use and the superior throwing range offered by their stick grenades, the lethality of German grenades was relatively low. The Mills, on the other hand, was devastating, even at distances of 100 metres.

In the close-quarter hand-to-hand fighting of the trenches, the hand grenade, or 'bomb' as it was popularly known, became the infantry weapon of choice. The platoon had a dedicated ten-man section solely charged with using the grenade. Unsurprisingly, these men, known as 'bombers', tended to be strong of arm and accurate throwers. For longer range work, rifle grenades provided the platoon with its own organic 'artillery' support and a ten-man section was trained in the use of this technically difficult weapon. The rifle, now relegated to a supporting role, was still an important element in manoeuvre warfare. The rifle section of ten men was used in support of the machine-gun to suppress enemy positions by fire and to manoeuvre around the enemy's flanks. This tactical structure and the techniques associated with it were still in their infancy in July 1916, but had become the core of the infantry war by 1918.

# Bayonets

Yesterday, two of our pigeons failed to return.
Note use of the bayonet as a cooking implement.
AWM ART02555

While the bayonet was a common weapon in World War One, its use was probably more psychological than practical. Veterans tended to play down the importance of the bayonet as a weapon, commenting, perhaps tongue-in-cheek, that it was more useful as a tool for routine tasks such as cooking, opening cans, tent pegging, digging, as a trench clothes hook, etc.

The British and, therefore, the Australian armies in the early period of World War One, were strong advocates of aggressive patrolling and bayonet charges. However, at Gallipoli the Anzacs soon learnt that a bayonet on the end of a Lee-Enfield rifle was not an ideal weapon for trench warfare. The rifle and bayonet combination proved too long for some trench systems and a strike at the chest tended to stick in the enemy's breastbone or ribs, whereas the pain from a stomach or groin wound usually had the enemy soldier grasp the blade and attempt to wrest control of the weapon from his opponent. The Anzacs quickly developed their own arsenal of trench-fighting weapons including improvised clubs, blades or knuckledusters.

# German *Seitengewehr* 98/05 'Butcher Blade' Bayonet

The German *Seitengewehr* 98/05 bayonet was the most common bayonet used by the German military during World War One. Nicknamed the 'butcher blade' by the Allies because of its distinctive shape, it was both a practical tool and bayonet. Various versions evolved over the war, including a 'saw back' model which was designed to be used as a tool but concerned the Allies so much that they threatened to kill or torture any German soldier captured with one.

German bayonet types. (Photo courtesy of the Australian Army Infantry Museum)

# British Pattern 1907 (P.07) Bayonet

Standard British pattern bayonet. AWM 07076.

The P.07 was the standard issue bayonet for the Lee-Enfield rifle for all Commonwealth forces during World War One. It was about half a metre long with two variations used by Australian troops at the Battle at Fromelles: the hooked quillon and straight guard types (photo is of a hooked quillon type). The P.07 was plain but practical and an effective weapon and tool.

British and Australian equipment (essentially the same) was generally the equal of its German counterpart. The standard British issue rifle for infantry was the .303 short magazine Lee-Enfield rifle. The rifle was sturdy, accurate and reliable, but too long for use in the confined space of trenches and bunkers. For trench-raiding, more basic weaponry, including knuckledusters, knives and clubs, was employed as stealth was as important as effectiveness. In an attack, the hand grenade became the weapon of choice for both attackers and defenders as it enabled the enemy to be engaged without exposing the user to enemy fire. The extension of the hand grenade concept, the rifle grenade, became an important weapon, particularly during the later years of the war. The rifle grenade provided infantry with their own organic means of engaging difficult targets such as bunkers, pill boxes or machine-gun nests at a longer, and therefore safer, range. Machine-guns, with their high rate of fire, were excellent infantry weapons, but the medium weapons of the early years of the war were too heavy to be used by advancing infantry. It was the British adoption of the Lewis gun that first provided the infantry with a mobile machine-gun capability. First introduced into service in late 1915, the Lewis gun brought rapid change to both infantry assault tactics and organisation.

While the British Army had increased in strength ten-fold, this expansion was not achieved without cost. The biggest problem was the poor state of readiness of many of the new divisions in the BEF. Lack of equipment and trained instructional staff placed enormous pressure on the preparation of new formations for the front. Casualties and the huge expansion diluted the numbers of experienced staff officers and regimental leaders available to man the new formations. The training programs in Great Britain still bore little relevance to Western Front conditions, so many formations arrived at the front totally unprepared for trench warfare. Most of the new formations were sent to quiet parts of the line, called 'nurseries', to give them some experience before they were involved in anything as complex as an organised attack. In July 1916, with the demands of the Somme, there were insufficient divisions available to allow this system to continue. The BEF still tried to send new and untried divisions to the three armies not involved in the Somme but this meant that, when one of these armies was required to mount an offensive action, it lacked the experienced troops necessary.

When the Australian divisions arrived in France in mid-1916 (the 5th Division Headquarters recommended operations on 25 June), they were unimpressed to discover that the High Command did not consider their experience at Gallipoli as adequate preparation for the Western Front. They soon understood why this view prevailed and their own experiences quickly taught them the veracity of the High Command view. The Australian divisions enjoyed some advantages 63 over their British counterparts. As they had not yet been heavily involved in battle, they were close to their authorised strength and the 5th Division entered the Battle of Fromelles at full strength. The Australian division followed the standard organisation of a British division and was under-strength only in some specialist areas such as gunners, trench mortar crews, pioneers and engineers. In many cases, the 'specialists' were present but insufficiently trained.

## Rifle, SMLE 0.303-inch, No. 1, Mk III*

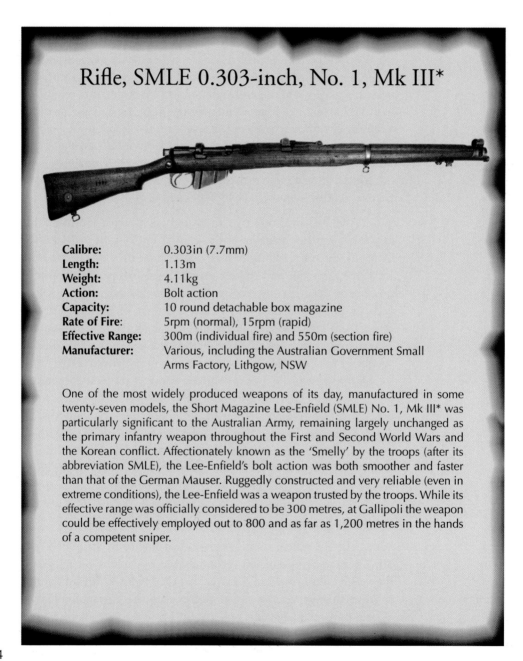

| | |
|---|---|
| **Calibre:** | 0.303in (7.7mm) |
| **Length:** | 1.13m |
| **Weight:** | 4.11kg |
| **Action:** | Bolt action |
| **Capacity:** | 10 round detachable box magazine |
| **Rate of Fire:** | 5rpm (normal), 15rpm (rapid) |
| **Effective Range:** | 300m (individual fire) and 550m (section fire) |
| **Manufacturer:** | Various, including the Australian Government Small Arms Factory, Lithgow, NSW |

One of the most widely produced weapons of its day, manufactured in some twenty-seven models, the Short Magazine Lee-Enfield (SMLE) No. 1, Mk III* was particularly significant to the Australian Army, remaining largely unchanged as the primary infantry weapon throughout the First and Second World Wars and the Korean conflict. Affectionately known as the 'Smelly' by the troops (after its abbreviation SMLE), the Lee-Enfield's bolt action was both smoother and faster than that of the German Mauser. Ruggedly constructed and very reliable (even in extreme conditions), the Lee-Enfield was a weapon trusted by the troops. While its effective range was officially considered to be 300 metres, at Gallipoli the weapon could be effectively employed out to 800 and as far as 1,200 metres in the hands of a competent sniper.

# Grenade, Mills Patent, Hand, No. 5

The 'Mills Bomb' was a simple, rugged and effective hand grenade and arguably the best known of all those used in World War One. At the start of the war, Britain lacked an effective grenade and troops often resorted to the use of home-made 'jam tin' bombs. Initially, the British High Command regarded the hand grenade as somewhat extraneous. The No. 5 Mills Bomb was introduced in May 1915 and, by Fromelles, it was the standard grenade on issue to the Australians. The Mills Bomb was a fragmentation bomb — it had a serrated exterior case and produced numerous fragments on exploding. In 1917 an improved version, the No. 36M, was introduced. It remained the standard British and Commonwealth grenade for fifty years.

The 5th Australian Division had been formed in Egypt in February 1916, part of the process that saw the AIF expand from two infantry divisions to five. The Light Horse provided the core for another two mounted divisions which remained in the Middle East until the end of the war. The 4th and 5th Divisions were created by simply splitting the original sixteen battalions of the AIF in two and bringing the resulting thirty-two battalions up to strength with the large numbers of unattached reinforcements then in Egypt. The 4th and 8th Brigades, which were already in Egypt, provided the remaining battalions. While this diluted the battle-hardened original battalions, it ensured the majority of the AIF's infantry battalions had some combat veterans in the ranks to stiffen the novices. The 5th Division received only basic training in Egypt before moving to France. Most of this training centred on fitness, small unit tactics and musketry. The division lacked adequate stocks of artillery or access to modern technology such as aircraft or trench mortars and, consequently, scope for larger formation and combined arms training was non-existent. Thus the division arrived in France largely ignorant of the basics of the new style of warfare.

# Light Machine-Gun, 0.303-inch, Lewis Mk1

| | |
|---|---|
| **Calibre:** | 0.303in |
| **Length:** | 1.28m |
| **Weight:** | 12.7kg (empty), 14.9kg (loaded) |
| **Action:** | Gas, automatic fire, air-cooled, magazine fed, bipod mount |
| **Rate of Fire:** | 500-600rpm (cyclic). Normal: bursts of 4–5 rounds as required. Rapid: 120rpm. |
| **Capacity:** | 47 and 97 round drum magazine |
| **Effective Range:** | 550m; on bipod: 800m; max: 3200m |
| **Manufacturer:** | Birmingham Small Arms Co. |

The Lewis gun entered production in the UK in early 1914 and was accepted for British military service in 1915. One advantage of the Lewis over other machine-guns of the time, such as the Vickers, was that it could be carried and fired by one man. This allowed more flexibility in its use and allocation and it quickly became the standard infantry light machine-gun of the British and Australian armies. It was also employed as an anti-aircraft gun and as an armament on British aircraft and the Mk IV tank. Reliable and relatively easy to use, the Lewis gun was a common sight on the Western Front — even the Germans used captured Lewis guns. By the end of the war, over 50,000 Lewis guns had been produced, outnumbering the Vickers by a ratio of 3:1.

The British contribution to the Battle of Fromelles was the 61st (2nd South Midland) Division — also not a battle-hardened, experienced formation. As its name suggests, the 61st was the second division to be raised in the South Midlands. At the outbreak of war in August 1914, the War Office had issued instructions that the Territorial Force (the equivalent of Australia's militia) should form a force of men prepared to serve overseas and a second force of men for 'home service only' who would constitute the reserve element and receive and train new recruits. In the South Midlands, the 48th Division became the first-line overseas service division and left for France in March 1915. The 'home service only' formation, named the 61st Division in April 1915, despite suffering equipment shortages and a lack of training, continued to receive and despatch groups of reinforcements to France throughout 1915. The division's best troops were continually lost to other units and consequently it never achieved high levels of combat preparedness.

With the demand for manpower outstripping supply, even the home service divisions had to be prepared for service at the front. In February 1916 the 61st Division moved to Salisbury Plain to commence pre-deployment training. On 21 May, the anticipated move to France occurred, with the division first concentrating in the reserve areas behind the line in northern France. Assigned to XI Corps, First Army, the division relieved the 38th (Welsh) Division in early June 1916, taking over the same part of the line from which the attack on Fromelles would be launched less than two months later. The division had little time to become familiar with the front, as it was tasked almost immediately with launching a series of bloody trench raids. While most were defeated by the defenders, some of the raiders did manage to penetrate the defences on occasion, thus providing the division with some experience of storming defended enemy positions — experience the 5th Australian Division sorely lacked.

## The French Army of 1916

The French Army was the core of the Allied military effort on the Western Front throughout the war. In the first two years of fighting, the French Army carried the greatest responsibility and had incurred more casualties by the middle of July 1916 than the British Empire was to incur during the whole war. Like the British, the French Army conducted military operations outside the main Western Front theatre, including at Gallipoli and Salonika but, understandably, the Western Front remained the major focus of French military effort.

For the first two years of the war, the French Army was larger, better trained, better equipped and better led than its British ally. Although its confidence had been dented by the setbacks in the early battles of the war, especially the offensive attacks on the southern end of the front line known as the Battles of the Frontiers in August and September 1914, the French Army did not disintegrate but conducted a campaign of hard-fought offensives throughout 1915. Even the dreadful losses at Verdun did not destroy French military capability or willingness to fight.

Organisationally, the French Army followed a typical European pattern. The basic infantry combat element was the infantry division; two or more divisions then became a corps. Corps were assembled into armies then army groups. Within the division, the infantry elements were initially contained in two or three infantry regiments, sometimes with an additional reserve regiment and a *chasseur* group of one or two light infantry battalions. By 1916, the reserve regiment had been removed and the *chasseurs* formed into their own divisions. Artillery was represented by three artillery groups (not formed regiments but rather groupings drawn from different regiments with different calibre weapons) and, from 1916, an additional 'trench artillery' battery with trench mortars of differing calibres. In 1914, each division still possessed its own organic cavalry of one squadron if part of a corps, or two squadrons if an independent division. Each division also had the usual range of support elements, including an engineer company and medical, administrative and logistics support troops. By 1916, specialist signals troops, mining and tunnelling engineers and increased medical support had been added.

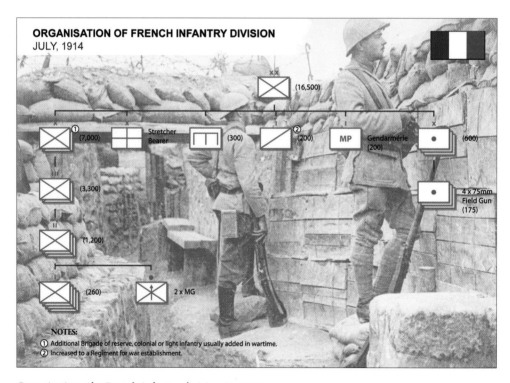

Organisation of a French infantry division in 1914.
(Mark Wahlert)

In 1914, the French Army fielded seventy-one infantry and ten cavalry divisions plus an alpine group in continental France. Large numbers of French colonial troops added to their numbers. Most of these arrived as battalions or regiments and were either sent as reinforcements to existing divisions or, more usually, grouped into new divisions. Most of the exotic troops in the French Army, including Zouaves, Tirailleurs and the Foreign Legion came from France's colonies. Some, especially the Zouave regiments early in the war, possessed a reputation for ferocity unmatched by the regular troops.

French equipment was generally inferior to its German equivalent, albeit not markedly so. France's most celebrated piece of military technology, the 75mm field gun, had a shorter range and a lighter shell than the equivalent German 77mm field gun which caused heavy casualties among French gunners early in the war. The French gun's greatest advantage was its rapid rate of fire, useful in manoeuvre warfare but of less importance in the static war now being fought. The equivalent British gun, the 18-pounder, was the best performer in terms of shell weight, firing an 8.4 kilogram shell, compared with the German gun's 6.85 kilogram and the French 6.2 kilogram. The French Army's most telling disadvantage, however, was not technological inferiority, but German numerical superiority. France had fewer soldiers, artillery pieces, machine-guns, hand grenades and factories to produce additional stocks. Following the German invasion, France lost access to half its coal resources and two-thirds of its iron and steel industries. Yet, despite these severe setbacks, France still managed to restructure its war industries and supply arms and equipment not only to its own forces but to the British, Belgians, Russians and eventually the Americans. To achieve this during a high attrition war was a major success for the French, something that is frequently overlooked or underplayed in English language accounts of the war. However, no amount of reorganisation or reconstruction could alter the disparity in numbers of soldiers. France had to look to her allies to redress the numerical disadvantage.

Like most continental armies, the French Army was conscript based. At twenty years of age, every French male became liable for three years' military service, with an ongoing training obligation of eleven years in the reserve and a further seven years in the Territorial Reserve once his full-time service ended. This provided a vast pool of trained manpower and, when coupled with an efficient call-up system, enabled France to mobilise an army of 2, 994,000 on the outbreak of hostilities. Most men served in the infantry while service in the artillery and engineers was mainly reserved for men from the railways, public works departments, shipyards or the telecommunications industry. The French Army was divided into three distinct groups: the metropolitan forces, the regular forces throughout the Empire and the locally raised Imperial troops in the colonies.

# The German Army of 1916

The organisation of the German Army reflected the political structure of the German state. Not unlike the British Army it faced, the German Army comprised troops from differing national origins under the operational control of the dominant Prussian High Command. Troops from the larger German states such as Prussia, Bavaria, Saxony and Württemberg all maintained their sense of origin while serving as an integral part of the 'German Army'. Each retained small distinctions on uniforms or minor pieces of equipment as points of identity. German senior commanders were not all Prussian; a number of these commanders had come originally from the high commands of other states. Despite this, only Bavaria maintained sufficient numbers of troops in service to be considered a true partner in the Prussian-dominated army for the duration of the war.

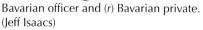
Bavarian officer and (r) Bavarian private.
(Jeff Isaacs)

Under the terms of the *Friedensprüsenzstärke* (peace strength) Law of June 1913, the peacetime strength and composition of the German Army was to be:

| State | Numbers |
|---|---|
| Prussia | 513,068 |
| Bavaria | 73,168 |
| Saxony | 49,472 |
| Württemberg | 25,468 |
| **Total** | 661,176 |

*Source:* AIF Military Pamphlet, *Notes on the German Army,* Government Printer, Melbourne, n. d., p. 17.

However, by 1 October 1913, the actual strength of the German Army had reached 793,280.

The German Army, like the French, was based on national service. All German males aged between seventeen and forty-five years of age were liable for military service, although some occupations were automatically exempt, even during time of war. There were four categories of military service: active, reserve, *Landwehr* and *Landsturm*. At the age of twenty, a male was required to undertake two years' active service (if infantry) or three years (if cavalry or field artillery). Following active service, four to five years' reserve service was required with another eleven in the *Landwehr* and seven in the *Landsturm*. The training obligation in the reserve and later categories was not onerous: the reserve requirement, for example, was two weeks full-time per year. In 1900, another category, the *Ersatz* reserve, was formed, consisting of men either fit for military service but exempt, or of men who could not be accommodated in the training units. The benefit of this category lay mainly in its ability to locate and organise reservists in a national call-up. Unlike the French, the rapidly growing German population proved a headache for German military authorities who had too many potential conscripts and little prospect of properly training them all. In part, the large number of reserve or *Ersatz* divisions in the German Army order of battle is a reflection of this problem. Conscription enabled the German Army to commence the war with over 840,000 troops already in service and over three million available for immediate return to the colours.

The German Army went to war with an entirely conventional structure. Like the French, the Germans were very experienced in the creation and command of large formations, routinely manoeuvring corps and army groups. The infantry division was the traditional central combat element and, like the French, the German division was built on a 'two' structure: two infantry brigades which in turn consisted of two infantry regiments, and a field artillery brigade which comprised two field regiments containing two *abteilung* (in this context, an *abteilung* is a battalion).

71

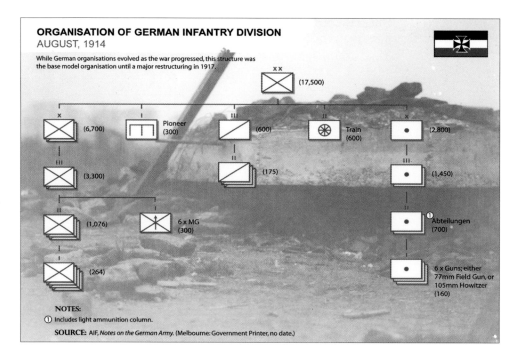

**ORGANISATION OF GERMAN INFANTRY DIVISION**
AUGUST, 1914

While German organisations evolved as the war progressed, this structure was the base model organisation until a major restructuring in 1917.

xx (17,500)

x (6,700) | Pioneer (300) | (600) | Train (600) | x (2,800)

(3,300) | (175) | (1,450)

(1,076) | 6 x MG (300) | ① Abteilungen (700)

(264) | 6 x Guns; either 77mm Field Gun, or 105mm Howitzer (160)

NOTES:
① Includes light ammunition column.

**SOURCE:** AIF, *Notes on the German Army*. (Melbourne: Government Printer, no date.)

Organisation of a German infantry division.
(Mark Wahlert)

The German Army was also conventionally equipped. The infantryman's basic weapon was the reliable Mauser rifle, Model 1898. Weighing 4.1 kilograms and 1.25 metres long, the weapon was designed for manoeuvre warfare in the open and suffered the same limitations in trench-fighting as the equivalent weapons of the French and British. For the same reasons, the Germans quickly adopted cruder but more effective hand-to-hand weapons for trench-fighting, including the famous 'stick' grenade. By 1916, the grenade had evolved and there were several variants including some without the 'stick'. The iconic German leather helmet or *pickelhaube* was as useless on the battlefield as the British cloth cap and by 1916 had been replaced by a steel helmet. One weapon whose value the Germans quickly recognised and used to great effect was the machine-gun. The standard German machine-gun of the war — which was still in service in 1942 — was the *Maschinengewehr* 08, or MG08. Very similar in operation to its British counterpart, the 7.92mm MG08 could fire up to 400 rounds per minute in sustained fire, with an effective range of over 2,000 metres and a maximum range of up to 3,600 metres. The MG08 was water-cooled like the Vickers, but could still overheat if fired for too long. It was a heavy weapon which severely restricted its mobility and German attempts to develop a lighter version were unsuccessful. The Germans began the war with approximately 12,000 MG08 in service and, by 1917, were producing over 14,000 per month.

German helmets – the *pickelhaube* is made of leather. In trench warfare, the steel helmet was more practical. (Photos courtesy of Captain John Land of the Australian Army Infantry Museum)

# Rifle, Mauser *Gewehr*, 98

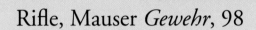

| | |
|---|---|
| **Calibre:** | 7.92mm |
| **Length:** | 1.25m |
| **Weight:** | 4.1kg empty |
| **Action:** | Bolt action |
| **Capacity:** | 5 round fixed box magazine |
| **Rate of Fire**: | 5rpm (normal), 15rpm (rapid) |
| **Effective Range:** | 300m (individual fire) and 500m (section fire) |
| **Manufacturer:** | Waffenfabrik Mauser, Deutsche Waffen und Munitionsfabriken and others under licence abroad |

The Mauser *Gewehr* model 1898 rifle, also known as Gew.98 or G98, was an evolution of previous Mauser rifle designs and the standard German infantry rifle throughout World War One. The G98 was a manually operated, magazine-fed, bolt action rifle. The bolt action was arguably the most notable feature of Mauser rifles of the period — it was simple, extremely strong and well designed, and became the standard to which other rifle manufacturers aspired. The Mauser could fire rifle grenades and came with a *Seitengewehr* 98/05 'butcher blade' bayonet. From late 1915, a number of G98 rifles were fitted with telescopic sights for sniper use. Because the length of the G98 made it unsuitable for trench warfare, a shorter, carbine model (the K98a) was also issued to assault units. The standard German infantry rifle for the Second World War, the *Karabiner* 98k, was a shortened and modified version of the G98 which it replaced in 1935.

The other new infantry weapon the Germans were quick to exploit was the mortar — the *minenwerfer* or 'mine thrower'. After studying the Russo–Japanese War and the siege of Port Arthur, the Germans quickly recognised the benefits of a short range, high trajectory weapon to attack small fortified positions and destroy barbed wire. Their experimentation eventually resulted in the development of a rifled, short-barrelled muzzle-loading, low-velocity weapon in three separate calibres and weights. With the low pressures involved, different types of explosives could be used and the comparatively high explosive weights delivered by this method made the trench mortar a formidable weapon in trench warfare. The heaviest, with a 25-centimetre calibre and firing a projectile weighing up to 100 kilograms, was first developed in 1910. The German Army had forty-four such weapons in service at the beginning of the war. They also developed another very light weapon, the *granatenwurfer*, a 'grenade thrower' which could project a two-kilogram grenade about 300 metres.

## German *Stielhandgranate* Grenade

Unlike their British adversary, the German Army developed and produced numerous types of grenades throughout World War One. These included the *Stielhandgranate* (stick grenade), the *Diskushandgranate* (disc grenade), *Eierhandgranate* (hand grenade) and *Kugelhandgranate* (ball grenade). The *Stielhandgranate* (stick grenade) proved the most popular among German soldiers and were either impact-detonated or time-fused (5.5 or 7-second delay). The grenades were usually carried in satchels around the soldier's neck.

# Medium Machine-gun,
## *Maschinengewehr* 08/15

**Calibre:** 7.92mm Mauser
**Length:** 1.175m
**Weight:** 26.5kg gun body, 4kg water, 38.5kg tripod
**Action:** Recoil
**Rate of fire:** Cyclic – 450rpm
**Feed system:** 250 round cloth belt
**Effective Range:** 2000m (max on tripod mount 3600m)
**Manufacturer:** Deutsche Waffen und Munitionsfabriken (DWM) and Spandau Arsenal, Germany

The *Maschinengewehr* 08 (MG08) Maxim machine-gun was almost a copy of Hiram S. Maxim's original 1884 Maxim gun. It was a bulky, heavy, short recoil operated, water-cooled, fully automatic belt-fed machine-gun. Using a separate attachment sight with range calculator for indirect fire, the MG08 was often operated from cover behind the forward German trench-line. The MG08 was usually issued on a sled-type mount of adjustable height (*SchlittenLafette* 08). This mount allowed the gun to be dragged through the battlefield or carried like a stretcher by two or more soldiers. The mount was provided with traverse and elevation mechanisms with rough and fine adjustments. Alternatively, the MG08 could be installed on a tripod mount commercially developed by DWM. One of Germany's most important weapons in World War One, it was ubiquitous on the Western Front in 1916, with 3,000 units produced each month in that year. By the Battle of Fromelles, the German Army had established a deadly network of machine-gun posts in front of the British line, using a combination of enfilade, indirect and direct fire, and intersecting arcs with riflemen support.

The *6th Bavarian Reserve Infantry Division* was a standard German line infantry division. Formed in September 1914, mainly from reservists but with a sprinkling of volunteers, the division fought at First Ypres and in the running battles now known as 'the race to the sea'. It boasted the standard German organisation with two infantry brigades, a cavalry regiment, a field artillery regiment, a foot artillery regiment and a pioneer company.

Unlike its British or Australian opponents at Fromelles, the *6th Bavarian Division* had occupied its defensive positions on Aubers Ridge for over a year and knew the terrain intimately. The Germans had fought the British in the same area a year earlier and, recognising the vulnerability of their sandbag breastwork fortifications to heavy artillery, had reinforced their lines with steel and concrete strong points and shelters. *Minenwerfer* sites featuring deep bunkers, strong overhead protection and small apertures were dug immediately behind their front lines. Almost impossible to locate, let alone destroy, these defensive positions posed a serious problem for the attacking troops in July 1916.

## German Defences

When the British and Australians attacked the Bavarian position, they were confronted by an evolving defensive system that quickly and systematically applied the lessons of previous battles. The Germans did not plan these trenches as temporary bulwarks; they viewed them as the borders of the new, greater Germany. Thus they were designed and built to fortress standard, constructed on a scale and quality unmatched by their opponents. The defences of each area were specifically designed to take advantage of the existing strengths of the site, either capitalising on possession of the high ground or integrating a river or canal into the defensive system.

While occupation of the high ground gave them a decided advantage, Aubers Ridge was not so dominant that the Germans could afford to neglect its development. From the German perspective, the protection it afforded the strategically important city of Lille marked it as the potential target of a major Allied attack at some stage. Consequently, the Aubers Ridge sector was highly developed as a defensive position. Unlike the Allies, the Germans harboured few concerns for the local inhabitants and exploited fully every resource they could employ to reinforce the position. A British officer's post-war survey of the sector recorded: 'all the material and mechanical advantages of Lille were exploited for the purposes of war by the

Germans. The electric tram system was diverted, electric power was diverted to the front line and used for many purposes, amongst which may be cited universal electric lighting of dugouts and the installation of powerful pumps for the drainage of the primeval swamp that the front line system soon resembled.' Prisoners of war and local French civilians were forced to work for long periods constructing trenches and fortifications.

Following the failure of some parts of their defensive systems in the 1915 battles, the Germans reorganised and developed an entirely new strategy during the early months of 1916. They began to construct a comprehensive 'defence-in-depth' with sophisticated support infrastructure including a well-protected communication network, supply and distribution chains using light rail, a solidly constructed road system and lengthy, well developed communication trench networks. The wholesale diversion of the civilian electric power supply enabled the German bunkers to be well lit, kept dry by pumping and artificially warmed. Concrete and steel began to replace wood and sandbags in the construction of strong points, machine-gun and mortar positions and bunkers. In the twelve months prior to the attack, the *6th Bavarian Reserve Division*, for example, installed one concrete and steel shell-proof shelter for every twenty-five metres of front line.

Most importantly, the Germans redesigned and restructured their defence lines. These positions no longer presented a hard crust that, when penetrated, lacked the depth to further impede the advance of the attacker. The German front now comprised three different zones: the *I Stellung*, the *hintergelende* and the *II Stellung*. The forward zone, the *I Stellung*, was to be the hard outer wall that forced the attacker to expend a major effort to reach and penetrate. When completed, this outer wall was to consist of several mutually supporting lines of breastworks, and was still being constructed when the attack was launched on 19 July. Old positions had been abandoned and new ones were being built to provide mutual support and create overlapping fire zones. As Peter Barton notes, Allied intelligence was confused by all these changes and assumed abandoned and largely destroyed German works were sound positions that could be converted to defensive points by the attacking British infantry.

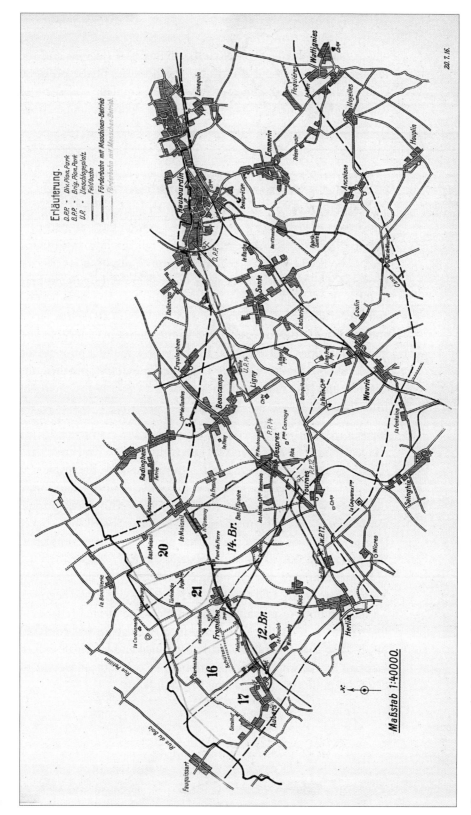

German transport infrastructure behind the German forward defensive zone. Map supplied as part of a report by Peter Barton on his research on behalf of the Australian Army in the *Hauptstaatsarchiv Kriegsarchiv* in Munich, Germany.

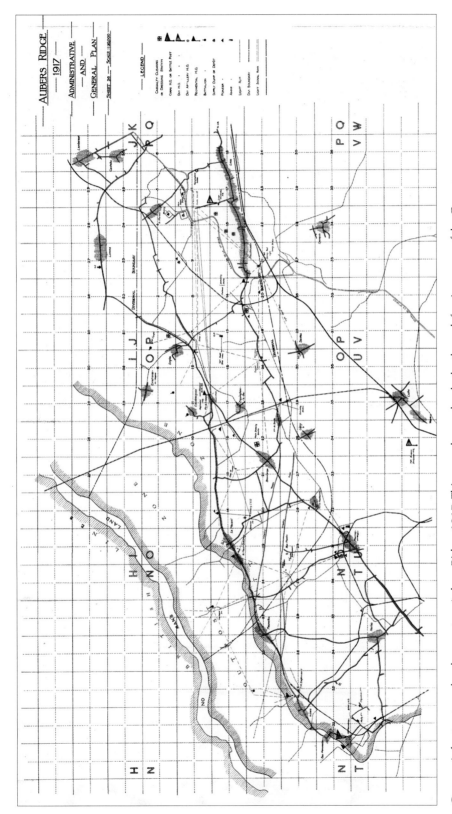

German infrastructure development on Aubers Ridge, 1917. This map shows clearly the three defensive zones of the German defence-in-depth concept. Map supplied as part of a report by Peter Barton on his research on behalf of the Australian Army in the *Hauptstaatsarchiv Kriegsarchiv* in Munich, Germany.

79

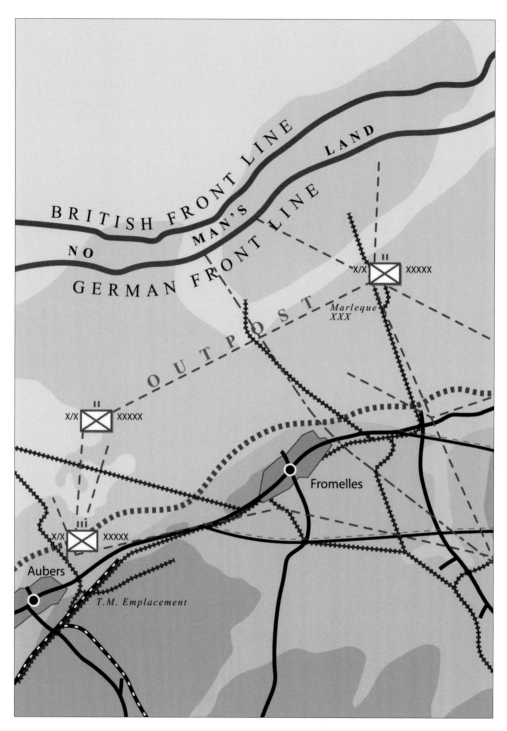

Defence-in-depth shown in this rendering of the German map. The dotted
line on Aubers Ridge is the second defence line. (Mark Wahlert)

The new concept of front line defence also included the construction of salients. These features could be seen clearly on any trench map of the German lines in France or Belgium in 1916. Salients were heavily fortified positions projecting out from the front-line trenches into No Man's Land. Their sole purpose was to allow the machine-gunners inside to fire along the lines of any infantry seeking to attack the trenches on either side of them. The two salients facing the British attack, the Sugarloaf and Wick salients, were formidable positions. Apart from the physical strength of their concrete and steel construction, the ability of the Germans to provide supporting machine-gun fire from the adjoining trenches and positions behind the front line on the higher ground and from artillery on and behind Aubers Ridge ensured that capturing them would be a major tactical achievement. This was not a task to assign to inexperienced and partially trained troops.

Map shows German machine-gun positions in the 5th Division zone illustrating the interlocking arcs of fire – green arrows. Map supplied as part of a report by Peter Barton on his research on behalf of the Australian Army in the *Hauptstaatsarchiv Kriegsarchiv* in Munich, Germany.

Should any attacker penetrate the *I Stellung*, the next line of defence, the *hintergelende*, was designed to further weaken and delay his advance. Constituting a scattered line of fortified, mutually supporting strong points — including farm houses and cottages as well as short fire trenches and specially constructed covered positions now known as pill boxes — all well sited to maximise interlocking arcs of fire, this line of defences was already well established by the time the attack began.

The third zone, the *II Stellung*, was even more strongly developed. It was sited at the top of the ridge which provided uninterrupted observation over all possible lines of advance. No attacker could approach it unobserved, while reinforcements and resupply could be sent into the *II Stellung* without being visible to the attacker (unless the attacker had aircraft in support). In Fromelles itself, *II Stellung* made use of the existing civilian infrastructure converting houses on the end of the ridge and the church into strong points and observation posts. Building the strong point inside an existing cottage or in the church ensured that it remained invisible to British artillery observers and thus escaped special treatment by the artillery prior to the attack.

Throughout the defence zone, an extensive network of well-constructed communication trenches enabled the Germans to move troops quickly between the zones and laterally across the battlefield. Deep trenches ran back up the face of the ridge and protected counter-attack forces being brought up during the battle. As a result, the attacking British and Australians faced a well-entrenched, confident enemy in a defensive position designed specifically to defeat the type of attack being launched. In the face of the formidable defences they encountered, the high casualty rate is perhaps less surprising than the attackers' limited degree of success in penetrating them.

# CHAPTER FOUR

# PLANNING FOR DISASTER:
## WHY WAS THE BATTLE OF
## FROMELLES FOUGHT?

Unlike the major set piece battles of the opening phases of the Somme when planning often occupied weeks or months, Fromelles was both a hastily planned opportunist battle and a reactive operation. It was opportunistic in that the High Command had long planned another limited offensive operation 'somewhere' to support the main thrust further south. This secondary offensive was to be launched to exploit the collapse of German resistance on the Somme which, at that time, seemed imminent. It was reactive because it was initiated to prevent the Germans moving reserves from the Lille part of the front to the Somme to reinforce their defences. Although plans for 'pinning' operations had been developed as part of the overall Somme plan, none had been formulated in any detail for any specific part of the line.

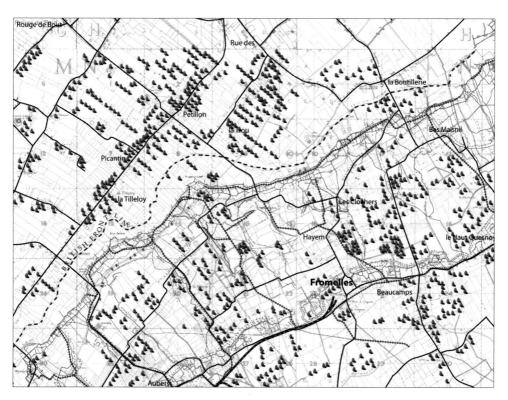

Overview map of the area, clearly showing in red the extensive German trench network on the forward slope of Aubers Ridge.
(Mark Wahlert)

This multiplicity of intentions makes it difficult to identify clear reasons for launching the Battle of Fromelles. The existence of another set of plans developed at the local command level further compounds this difficulty. All commanders at all levels plan for operations in their area of responsibility. They plan defensive operations based on various enemy attack options and potential problems in their own defences. They plan opportunistic offensive operations ready to be implemented at short notice to capitalise on surprise developments in the enemy's defensive situation. This type of planning, known as contingency planning, is standard military practice today. Major General Sir Richard Haking, Commander of XI Corps and the commander responsible for the sector of the front containing Fromelles, continuously developed plans for operations to capture various parts of the line, as did his counterparts all along the front line. Some modern commentators regard this sound military practice as evidence of some sort of obsession with Aubers Ridge. As the XI Corps diaries reveal, Haking also had plans for attacks on Vimy Ridge and other militarily important objectives within his area of responsibility. These plans, intended for both local tactical and strategic purposes, were immediately available to Haking's higher headquarters when the need for an attack was identified by BEF Headquarters.

The reasons advanced for attacking parts of the German line not involved in the Somme operation made sound military sense. The British High Command was convinced that the relentless attacks on the German lines on the Somme were exerting enormous pressure on the German Army. Verdun had already inflicted huge casualties on the Germans and the slow but continuous advance on the Somme was compounding these losses. The Germans faced something of a tactical dilemma: Falkenhayn had decreed that every inch of German-held ground was to be defended and, if lost, to be regained by counter-attack as soon as possible. This meant every British local success on the Somme had to be challenged and subjected to counter-attack. Falkenhayn's orders required the German defenders to make the same types of costly assaults on protected British infantry that the British had made on the opening day, with similar outcomes. The results of the German counter-attacks — high casualty counts for little tactical gain — paralleled the British experience.

Once British intelligence became convinced that the Germans were 'combing out' troops from quiet parts of their front to reinforce the Somme defenders, local Allied attacks to thwart this practice became inevitable. Denying the enemy such operational and strategic flexibility was a sound military tactic. In an attempt to pin German reserves in areas of the front remote from the focal points of Allied operations, Haig ordered his three unengaged army commanders to investigate limited attacks against quieter parts of the line to keep the Germans busy. The decision to use feints and widely dispersed attacks to pin enemy troops in areas away from the main attack was, at the time, both rational and defensible, irrespective of whether the intelligence assessment of German actions was later found to be correct, or whether the solution proposed to fix the military problem actually worked.

## The Strategic Reasoning behind the Fromelles Operation

The likely movement of German troops to reinforce the defenders on the Somme had been anticipated early in the planning stage by the Allied High Command. Planning to prevent this had also been ongoing in the lead-up to the Somme. Haig and Joffre had examined a number of possible feints to deny the Germans any tactical or operational flexibility. Concurrent with planning the main Somme attack, a number of other, preliminary feints had also been planned as early as January 1916 to deceive the enemy on the location of the main attack. While the unfolding events made these plans redundant, this planning provided Haig with some existing operational concepts that could be quickly converted to planned pinning operations.

There was another element in the combination of events that led to the decision to attack at Fromelles. Haig's original aim had been to launch his major offensive in Belgium, rather than on the Somme. When the arguments in favour of the Somme prevailed, he continued to examine options for more limited offensives in Belgium. Through most of the first half of 1916, his preferred location for a secondary operation was southern Belgium where the Germans had carved a great salient in the British line from south of Ypres to just south of Messines. Both Haig and Second Army Commander General Plumer were planning an offensive against this salient as late as June 1916.

Haig advised his commanders that, should the Germans weaken their defences in this sector by moving reinforcements south to the Somme, he would consider launching a new offensive rather than a diversionary attack in this area. Even at this early stage, the Australian divisions had been selected for the assault at Messines and the 2nd and 7th Australian Infantry Brigades were moved out of the line from the Armentières sector to the Messines sector in anticipation. However, the unanticipated heavy demands of the Somme campaign on both men and materiel, combined with the poorly developed logistics infrastructure behind the Messines sector, meant that Haig lacked the resources to commence and sustain even a reduced secondary offensive.

Although this second offensive did not eventuate, the planning that had been devoted to it provided compelling evidence to all Haig's senior commanders that he was looking for opportunities to broaden the fighting front through fresh limited offensives. In a command environment so demonstrably focused on the strategic offensive, thinking small was not a realistic option. Planning for any combat operation larger than small-scale raiding would always run the risk of being developed beyond simple tactical outcomes to strive for results that could hasten the end of the war.

On 5 July, Haig received some very optimistic intelligence assessments pointing to the imminent collapse of the Germans on the Somme. He immediately began to plan fresh attacks further away from the central point of anticipated enemy collapse that would both increase the pressure on the Germans and fully exploit any collapse. While hindsight has enabled Haig's legions of critics to condemn him for treating this as a credible assessment, at the time and under the circumstances, he was in no position to doubt what his specialists were telling him. Consequently, his planning of additional operations to fully exploit the potential collapse of part of his enemy's forces made good military sense then — as indeed it would today. Haig therefore asked the commanders of his First and Second Armies to 'select a front on which to attempt to make a break in the enemy's lines, and to widen it subsequently'. If the Germans should decide to abandon their defences on the Somme (as they did in February 1917), Haig was also keen to have additional attack plans in place to convert any withdrawal to a rout.

However, in 1916 the planning of subsidiary offensives was not universally accepted as sound strategy. The French Commander-in-Chief, General Joffre, also demanded that the British maintain their efforts on the Somme rather than planning fresh attacks elsewhere. Whether Joffre's opposition was based on an assessment of the BEF's capability, a desire to retain the destruction of the German Army in France as the priority, or a concern that a more remote operation might enable the Germans to reignite their attacks at Verdun, is unclear. What is clear, however, is that Joffre's demands ensured that Haig and BEF Headquarters remained firmly focused on the Somme.

The juxtaposition of these two operational concepts clearly highlights the dilemma that Haig was facing. He was undertaking an operation (the Somme attack) made necessary by the strategic situation but for which he himself believed his resources were inadequate. Yet he also wanted to initiate another attack which might end the war sooner. His direction to his army commanders to initiate planning for this subsidiary action effectively passed the dilemma to his subordinates. It thus became a question of judgement at army and even corps level as to whether the strategic risk of *not* undertaking the operation outweighed the prospects of failure. In the summer of 1916, all the British commanders undertaking any offensive operation faced this dilemma and its associated risks.

While preparations by Second Army in Belgium for its attack at Messines suggested the possibility of a subsidiary operation, this was ruled out by its commander, General Plumer, on the grounds that the enemy was showing no signs of weakening his defences. However, Plumer did accept that further south, where Second Army met First Army at a defensive feature in the German lines called the Sugarloaf, the enemy was reducing his defences and holding the front more lightly than elsewhere. He also believed that, while his army was not strong enough to mount an offensive on its own, if the task was shared by the two adjacent armies, sufficient resources could be assembled to provide some prospect of success. A third factor encouraging Plumer to propose an attack was that he knew Haking had already completed preliminary planning for an operation in the area. As much of the basic initial planning was thus complete, the time required to mount an operation was significantly reduced. On these grounds, on 8 July Plumer offered to make a joint arrangement with Lieutenant General Monro (see biographical notes), Commander of the First Army, to attempt a breakthrough. Arguably, therefore, it was General Plumer who finally initiated the chain of events that culminated in the Battle of Fromelles.

The timing of the prospective operation was also an issue and represented a different and separate military problem. Alongside optimistic reports of progress on the Somme, Haig was also being advised that German troop reinforcements were arriving on the Somme from other sectors. His initial response was to order his army commanders to increase their trench-raiding programs in an attempt to prevent further transfers by threatening the integrity of the overall German front line. The discovery that the *13th Jäger Battalion*, which had been garrisoning part of the line in the Fromelles sector, was fighting on the Somme provided justification for the proposed operation. The subsequent identification of a further nine battalions that had moved from Lille to the Somme focused Haig's attention on the Lille sector of the front line.

One direct consequence was a specific instruction issued to the Commander II Anzac Corps, Lieutenant General Sir Alexander Godley, to commence a program of vigorous trench-raiding — using much larger raiding parties than before — to prevent further transfers. On four successive nights from 9 July, the New Zealand Division mounted a number of sizeable raids, although none was successful in convincing the Germans that the integrity of their line was under serious threat. Clearly, something more convincing than raiding was necessary. A limited attack, with limited objectives to seize a part of the German front line, was the next step in escalation.

## Operational Background to the Fromelles Attack

Most critics hold Sir Richard Haking (see biographical notes), Commander of XI Corps and the designated local commander for the attack, personally responsible for the Fromelles disaster. Consequently, it is difficult to divorce the actual plan from the popular image of its planner: many published analyses of Fromelles begin their assessment with the presumption that the plan was flawed from the outset because it was Haking's plan.

Haking's critics, both then and now, portray him as a stupid, unfeeling bully and a liar. He is variously described as obsessed with an attack on Aubers Ridge and with continuing to hurl men into an attack that any 'reasonable observer' could see was already doomed. It is often stated or implied that he owed his continued employment and command to a close personal relationship with Haig. In fact it was Sir John French, Haig's predecessor, who promoted Haking to command XI Corps in September 1915.

Haking had his share of enemies within the British military establishment — a situation that was hardly unusual at the time. The senior British command was beset with rivalry and, apart from the issues of talent and ability, commanders often owed promotion and similar advancements to luck, patronage, family connections and membership of the right cliques. Many of the criticisms of Haking appear to emanate from subordinates whom he dismissed from active service. While some of his contemporaries did not regard him as the cleverest of the British corps commanders in France, others, including many of his military contemporaries, viewed him as an innovative thinker. His published ideas, in particular his work on company training developed while he was an instructor at Staff College before the war, still 'has a freshness about it and an insight into human characteristics that would not be out of place in a modern military work'. The fact that Haking was never promoted to army command during the war may point to his limitations or, conversely, illustrate how few promotion opportunities arose for officers close to the top of the BEF command pyramid. Whatever the causes or consequences of his decisions at Fromelles in July 1916, dismissing them as the actions of an unthinking fool is overly simplistic.

Before turning to the formulation of the plan itself, it is essential to address one final accusation against Haking — the view that the heavy casualties were a direct result of his obsession with capturing Aubers Ridge. As Patrick Lindsay comments, 'The driving force behind these unformed plans [to attack at Fromelles] was the same British general who had previously twice tried to take Aubers Ridge — both at enormous cost and both without success — Haking.' Apparently he had learned nothing from his previous disasters. He maintained his mindless and unjustified belief that an attacking force could overcome even the most entrenched defences provided it had the necessary 'will to succeed'. In view of the strictly limited objectives set in Haking's corps orders and his strong emphasis on adequate preparation of the objective by artillery, these are difficult charges to sustain. His late decision to reduce the size of the Fromelles attack from three divisions to two when the promised additional artillery support failed to materialise is further indication that he clearly understood what he was asking his troops to do and appreciated the difficulties they would face. The obsession claim, which probably originates with a speech given after the war by an Australian brigade commander — also of uncertain temperament and judgement — appears to be based on the fact that Haking continued to plan for the capture of Aubers Ridge following the failures of 1915.

Aubers Ridge did not suddenly rise to prominence in 1916. A series of battles had been fought for its possession by the French in October 1914 and the British in 1915. Apart from tactical considerations, Aubers Ridge formed an important salient in the Allied defensive line. The ridge dominated Lille and its surrounds — the most important industrial and natural resource area in France. Holding the ridge would deny the Germans the opportunity to exploit these resources. Aubers Ridge was therefore a strategic target of considerable significance. In 1915, the British fought three battles — Neuve Chapelle (10–12 March), Aubers Ridge (9 May–16 June) and Festubert (15 May) — in an attempt to capture the ridge. The battle for Aubers Ridge was fought in the area immediately adjoining the south-western end of the Fromelles battle zone. While each battle was different, the one factor they had in common was that, when well prepared by artillery, limited advances and occupation of the enemy's front line proved possible. These battles also showed that converting limited advances into a major breakthrough of an enemy position was an entirely more difficult task. Far from discouraging Haking in his planning for the Fromelles battle, these earlier actions demonstrated that limited objectives could be taken and that the enemy would be required to maintain sizeable forces to prevent any further exploitation of limited, localised successes. The battle also demonstrated that even limited success was a bloody affair and that casualties would be high. The Germans, too, learned from these battles, identifying in particular the weakness of the single trench-line defensive system at Neuve Chapelle. By the time of Fromelles, the Germans had developed a much more effective defence-in-depth approach based on multiple defensive trench-lines.

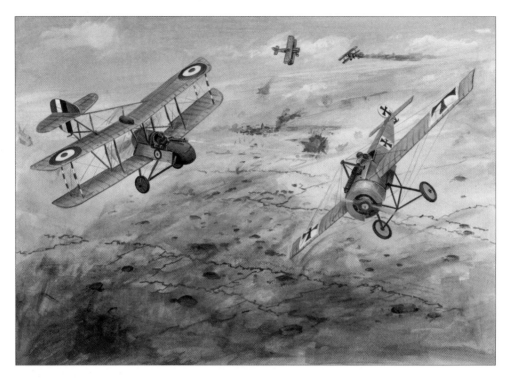

Aerial observation was becoming such a critical element of trench warfare that major effort was devoted to denying the airspace to enemy aircraft. (Jeff Isaacs)

The charge that Haking was 'obsessed' with capturing Aubers Ridge also fails to acknowledge standard military practice. Aubers Ridge was a target of particular, indeed strategic, significance. Any military commander seeking to inflict serious strategic damage on the German position in northern France would attempt to capture the ridge. Like Vimy Ridge further south, the dominance of Aubers Ridge over so much occupied French territory made it an important military target. It was for this reason that it attracted several attempts by both British and French forces to recapture it and why the Germans invested such significant resources in its defence. Unlike Vimy Ridge, Aubers Ridge remained firmly in German hands until close to the end of the war. Haking was not being 'obsessive' in focusing on a major strategic target within his zone of responsibility, he was doing his job. The reason he was never given the full authority or resources to achieve his goals was because his superiors, also doing their job, identified other, higher priority targets for attacks elsewhere and assigned their limited resources accordingly.

In June 1916, along with his fellow corps commanders in First and Second Army, Haking advanced a series of proposals for attacks within his corps sector. One proposal outlined an attack against a prominent German salient known as the Boar's Head, about seven kilometres south-west of the Sugarloaf. There were others, including his most ambitious suggestion for an operation against the Sugarloaf salient itself. 'I have also prepared an attack with a view to capturing and holding permanently 2,100 yards of the enemy's trenches from the Fauquissart Road at [map reference given] to the enemy's salient at [map reference of the Sugarloaf] between which points gas has been installed.' There is no evidence in this plan of an obsession with capturing the ridge itself. Haking's final version of the plan did include capture of the ridge if developments allowed, but this extension reflected the strategic aims of higher command. Indeed, according to the XI Corps war diary, this instruction came from Monro on 8 July 1916. Haking's original June outline plan more closely resembles the objectives given to the British 61st Division in the actual attack than later iterations with a broader focus.

Far from being obsessive, Haking's planning to attack enemy positions in his area of operations was standard military procedure and no less than what was expected by his superiors and subordinates. Planning for the reduction of an enemy feature that provides the enemy a defensive advantage is sound military practice. The Germans did not build salients into No Man's Land for appearances; they represented a major threat to the freedom of manoeuvre of the British forces in the area. Any commander with such a feature in his area of responsibility would develop different plans aimed at eliminating it when the opportunity arose.

The same arguments related to so-called 'line-straightening' operations. Never popular with the troops tasked to conduct them, such attacks were essential to strengthen defensive positions and prepare the ground for future offensive operations. They were almost invariably tactically justifiable at the time, even if severely criticised later for the casualties they incurred (especially if they were unsuccessful). In the case of Haking's plans for the elimination of a major defensive position such as the Sugarloaf, such an attack would have had the additional effect of compelling the Germans to retain sufficient forces in the area to recapture and defend the feature. Plumer and Second Army were quite prepared to support this operation.

Planning for a more substantial operation in the Fromelles sector continued in the aftermath of the less than successful raids and artillery harassing programs. Commanders at all levels in First Army began to recognise that something more convincing than trench-raiding was required. Among the plans advanced to the Commander

91

First Army was Haking's revised plan for his capture of a section of the German trenches west of the Sugarloaf, expanded to include a target the Germans would take seriously — the ridge from Aubers to Fromelles. Monro at first rejected even this revised plan, not because it was militarily unsound, but because he wanted to seize objectives such as Hill 70 near Loos, or Vimy Ridge. These objectives, closer to the anticipated breakthrough on the Somme, were regarded as offering greater tactical support to the pursuers of a retreating German Army. Haking was not advised that his revised plan had been rejected until 12 July, seven days prior to the attack on which it was based.

On the Somme, however, preparations were completed for the second phase attack, due to begin on 14 July. Once more, Haig and his planners were concerned by reports that the Germans were transferring troops to augment the Somme defenders. Consequently, they again looked to the First and Second Army sectors for operations that would prevent the Germans relocating troops. At first, they were attracted to the several existing proposals for 'artillery demonstrations' despite the evidence that such half-hearted actions were insufficient to deceive the Germans. It is surprising, in view of the artillery failures on the Somme, that the planning staff persisted with the belief that an artillery demonstration on its own would inflict convincing damage on the enemy's positions. It could be done, as previous battles such as Neuve Chapelle in 1915 had demonstrated, and as the 14 July attack on the Somme would also show, but only if conducted with a large number of guns, particularly heavy artillery. One demonstration plan for the Fromelles sector required the two adjacent armies to assemble a force of 360 light field guns and howitzers (the equivalent of six divisions' artillery assets) and some heavier artillery. This number of guns was simply insufficient to inflict enough damage to be convincing. Indeed, the total was smaller than the number of guns finally assembled to support the later plan including the infantry attack. Eventually, the planners accepted that something more akin to a conventional assault was the only demonstration that was likely to succeed in forcing the Germans to maintain their troop numbers in the sector.

The delays caused by these debates quickly prompted Haig's headquarters to become directly involved in the decision-making process. On 13 July, Major General R.H.K. Butler, Haig's Chief Operations Officer and Deputy Chief of Staff, was despatched to Monro's headquarters to precipitate a decision on some form of action. The shortcomings of the 'artillery only' idea were acknowledged and Butler agreed with the Chiefs of Staff of the two armies that a combined artillery/infantry demonstration was required. The proposal of a few days earlier — that First Army provide two infantry divisions for the task and Second Army one — was also adopted. The artillery of both the divisions involved, plus those from additional and surrounding formations, would begin preparatory shelling of the objectives the following day, using what guns were available and integrating new artillery support into the fire plan as it arrived. The infantry would begin their attack three days later, on 17 July.

Yet these decisions did not dispel the lingering confusion. On 16 July, Major General Butler again visited First Army Headquarters and informed Monro, in the presence of Generals Plumer and Haking, that there was 'no urgent need' for the XI Corps operation. He informed them that Haig did not wish the attack to take place unless the commanders on the spot were satisfied that their resources were adequate. In other words, Haig was now neither insisting the attack happen nor cancelling it. Both Monro and Haking — and presumably Plumer — believed they had the resources to successfully conduct the limited attack planned, so they opposed cancellation or deferral. Critics have seized on this decision as proof that the commanders involved, particularly Haking, were driven by ambition and unconcerned at the prospect of incurring unnecessary casualties among their men.

But there is another explanation. There was no suggestion that the intelligence assessment of the situation on the Somme was recognised as flawed at this stage, so the assumptions that led to the plan's initial development remained valid. This was an opportunity to inflict another blow on the enemy and no good reasons had been advanced as to why this opportunity should be allowed to slip. The reasons the battle ultimately failed were not yet obvious, and the casualties had not yet been incurred. Rather than question why the battle proceeded, critics of the action should explain what factors existed to justify its cancellation at this point, especially in the context of what was happening further south.

An operation of this size could only have been initiated so quickly if the necessary preplanning — including the survey and mapping of the enemy's positions; intelligence estimates of the enemy's strength; examination of the terrain and identification of artillery targets — had already been completed. As Haking had been developing options for the chosen area for months, his plans provided the only means by which an operation involving two separate commands could be undertaken quickly with any hope of success. Butler agreed that more artillery and additional supplies of shells would be required for a convincing artillery demonstration and these were duly promised. BEF Headquarters Order O.A.N. 4/35 advised of a special allotment to First Army of an additional 1,000 rounds of 60-pounder gun and 1,000 rounds of 9.2-inch howitzer ammunition to support this operation.

# Ordnance BL 9.2-inch Howitzer Mk 1

| | |
|---|---|
| **Calibre:** | 234.7mm (9.2in) |
| **Weight:** | 12.2 tonnes |
| **Crew:** | Six |
| **Rate of Fire:** | 1rpm |
| **Effective Range:** | 9199m (in 1916) |
| **Manufacturer:** | Coventry Ordnance Works |

The howitzer was designed in 1910 and first saw action in France in early 1915. It was one of several types of British siege guns for the Somme offensive in 1916. However, its size, weight of shell and destructive power saw production increase and, by the end of 1916, the British Army had taken delivery of 230 of these guns. The Mk 1 was sturdy and well designed, with a hydro-pneumatic recoil system which proved very reliable. When movement was necessary, the gun was broken down into three wagon-loads. Due to its relatively short barrel, the gun had a habit of 'jumping' when fired. To counter this, a heavy 'earth box' was attached to the front of the gun to weigh it down. Its key role was against enemy strong points, communication and front-line trenches, deep fortifications and counter-battery fire. The 9.2-in howitzer equipped the Australian Siege Battery (the 55th). With a shell weight of 290lbs (132 kg) and a range of almost 10 kilometres, the 9.2-in howitzer was the largest artillery piece employed by the AIF and remains the largest artillery piece to have seen active service with the Royal Regiment of Australian Artillery. At over 12 tonnes, the 9.2-in howitzer was one of the more difficult guns to bring into action. It took as long as forty-eight hours to prepare a suitable platform in the mud near Ypres in 1917 before the gun itself was brought forward for deployment, a process which could take up to twelve hours. While an official rate of fire was not recorded, it is noted that one gun reportedly fired thirteen rounds in six minutes. Given that the gun had to be lowered to the horizontal to be loaded, this would have been an extreme and unsustainable rate of fire. A more reasonable rate was one round per minute.

A 9.2-in Howitzer of the 2nd Australian Siege Battery
in action. AWM E00693

First Army Order Number 100 of 15 July describes clearly the purpose of the operation: 'to prevent the enemy from moving troops southward to take part in the defence of the Somme'. The action was designed to create the impression of an impending offensive operation on a large scale. No-one believed the Germans would stop sending reinforcements south if the threatened attack did not look capable of making major territorial gains. It was at this point that some confusion entered the planning cycle. On the one hand, First Army made it clear that the enemy needed to be aware of the preparations — in other words, secrecy had to be sacrificed so as to sow doubt in the enemy's mind. Those involved in the attack who survived to comment on it later regarded this as a scandalous decision. This prior warning ensured that the faint hope of success lent by the element of surprise would be completely extinguished.

On the other hand, the orders produced for the operation stressed that a heavy bombardment planned for the day before which would target the enemy several miles to the south was intended to sow doubt as to the true focus of the attack. The expressed intention was to entice the enemy to move some of his limited artillery to the south and assist the attacking infantry. But not all units were briefed on the 'no secrecy' concept; the 5th Division artillery orders emphasised the need to conceal the number of guns actually involved and to prevent unnecessary movement that would signal the artillery build-up.

If the attack was merely to be the 'feint' originally planned, the direction that secrecy be abandoned was a reasonable, albeit high-risk tactic. The enemy's preparations would be unnecessary and unrewarded if the attack did not eventuate. The 'no secrecy' decision thus lends weight to the argument of those who insist the original intention was not to mount an infantry attack but merely threaten it. However, according to the Australian Official Historian, Charles Bean, on 14 July when Haking explained his plan to Major General James McCay, Commander of the 5th Australian Division — the division that would cooperate with his own corps in mounting the attack — he failed to impress on McCay that this was to be an infantry feint, perhaps because Haking himself was uncertain as to the final intention. Instead he identified the 6,000 metre section of the enemy's front line from the Fauquissart–Trivelet Road to a point opposite La Boutillerie as the objective of the attack. In the sequence of events, it is difficult to determine whether this was a deliberate change of plan or merely poor coordination between different planning groups.

To confuse further the planning and issuing of orders, Haking also received news that, not only was the artillery support he had been promised to be significantly reduced, the promised allocation of shells was likewise to be smaller. Much of his artillery support was now to be provided by partially trained and completely inexperienced gunners, half from the 4th and 5th Australian Divisions. The trench mortar elements of these two divisions were not trained at all and some had not even received their equipment. Consequently, their potential contribution to the fire support plan was extremely limited.

Faced with this setback, Haking (wisely, as Bean states) changed his plan and reduced the size of the attacking force to two divisions on a frontage also reduced by a third. He still expected each division to attack using all three of its brigades, side by side, in marked contrast to standard British practice of the time. The usual British attack employed two of a division's three brigades in the initial attack with the third acting as divisional reserve and as the reinforcement or exploitation force. For this attack, Haking committed all three brigades from each division although, within each brigade, only half the troops were to be allocated to the initial attack with the two remaining battalions in each brigade following the assault waves. As the orders noted, 'By this means, the numbers would be sufficient to carry out the limited objective laid down and fresh troops would be available, either to relieve the assaulting troops, repel counter-attacks or undertake fresh offensive operations if these were ordered.'

# Three-inch Stokes Trench Mortar, Mk I

| | |
|---|---|
| **Type:** | Light mortar |
| **Calibre:** | 81.2mm (3.2 in) |
| **Weight:** | 49kg |
| **Action:** | Trip |
| **Crew:** | Two |
| **Rate of Fire:** | 25rpm (maximum); 6 – 8rpm (sustained) |
| **Effective Range:** | Planning 86m (max 731m) |
| **Manufacturer:** | British arsenals and in Allied countries under licence |

Designed in early 1915 to match the German Army's *minenwerfer*, the Stokes mortar was named after its inventor, Sir Frederick Wilfred Scott Stokes. It was a simple weapon, based on designs that had been in use since the Napoleonic era. With a high angle and curved trajectory, the role of the mortar on the Western Front was to lob shells into trenches that remained largely unaffected by flat trajectory weapons such as artillery. By 1915 the Germans had deployed a large number of light *minenwerfer* ranging from 77mm to 150mm, as well as a number of larger calibre weapons. The British and French soon followed the German lead by developing and deploying their own heavy mortars. However, all of these mortars were relatively heavy 'trench artillery' and consequently less mobile. What was needed was a light mortar that could accompany the troops as they stormed enemy trench systems and provide immediate and direct fire support beyond rifle grenade range, especially to help repel the inevitable counter-attack. Such a mortar could also be used to destroy machine-gun nests. The Stokes mortar fitted this requirement well. A good crew could have six or more mortars in the air before the first had landed. As a weapon of surprise and shattering impact, the Stokes was probably only exceeded by the Livens Projector. The 3-in bomb was by no means as destructive as the German *minenwerfers* of various sizes, but for simplicity of transport and operation, as well as rate of fire, the Stokes was unsurpassed. Eventually almost 2,000 units were produced, only replaced in the late 1930s with the 3-in mortar (Ordnance ML 3-in mortar).

The constant modification and variation of the plan was a major problem for all involved. While many of the reasons for the changes were either beyond Haking's control or forced on him by external factors, it was still his responsibility to ensure that his plan was understood by all those involved, that sufficient time was allowed for orders to be drafted, printed and distributed and subordinate instructions, based on these orders, similarly finalised and circulated. A major consequence of the changes to the artillery allocation was its effect on the preparation program. This problem was further compounded by the weather. Between 16 and 18 July, there were thunderstorms, low cloud and mist, which meant very few air operations could be flown to assist artillery registration. Even on 19 July the mist did not clear until mid-morning, preventing major artillery registration earlier in the day.

By this stage of the war, no-one, even a commander such as Haking who included men's morale and offensive spirit in calculating combat readiness, was unaware of the critical need for complete artillery preparation of a fortified position before launching an infantry attack. Artillery fire plans were complex and required considerable skill from the gunners, especially in this instance where the front-line trenches were very close together in some areas. Haking was also planning a series of artillery feints in which the guns' barrage would target the front lines, then move ('lift' in gunners' jargon) to the rear areas, suggesting to the Germans that the attack had begun, before returning to the front line to catch the defenders manning the parapets. Given the complexity of the artillery requirement, good gunnery skills and a well-understood fire plan were the essential ingredients for success. In the rush to mount the operation and then add the last-minute changes, the time available for the artillery to modify, adapt and understand the revised fire plan was always going to be insufficient, especially for the unskilled gunners.

## Tactical Considerations

The basic tactical consideration for the planners was the location of the attack; at Fromelles the location chosen was a very difficult place to launch an attack. In fact, the plan could only have been more difficult had it included the necessity to prepare the attack in secrecy so as to ensure tactical surprise. Given that the jumping-off points, and all the lines of approach behind them, were in full view of German observers on Aubers Ridge, tactical surprise could only have been achieved if all preparations had been made at night and in silence. For troops new to the trench systems of the Western Front, this would have been almost impossible.

An old ditch turned into a trench that formed part of the objective of the 8th and 14th Australian Infantry Brigades in the attack on Fromelles on 19 July 1916. AWM E03971

The old No Man's Land of Fromelles battlefield viewed from the north-east corner of Sugarloaf Salient looking towards the line from which the 15th Australian Infantry Brigade began its attack on 19 July 1916. AWM E04030

The planners' main tactical considerations were the flatness of the terrain; the obstacles posed by a series of drainage ditches — including the Laies Brook — that criss-crossed No Man's Land; and the enemy's ability to observe the entire battlefield. The varying width of No Man's Land was an issue for timing in the attack phase while supply and reinforcement while under observed enemy fire once the objectives had been seized was another major concern.

One tactical problem that exercised the minds of the generals almost to the end was the question of how to exploit the capabilities of the infantry's best weapons: the Vickers gun, Lewis gun and the Stokes mortar. These weapons were considered so vital to the division's firepower that their loss could not be contemplated. Their best protection was to leave them behind in their original positions. However, moving them forward into the captured enemy trenches offered the best chance of consolidating and defending the gains made. Additionally, while the Lewis gun was a relatively simple weapon to move, the same was not true for either the mortar or the medium Vickers gun. Yet, of all three, the most effective weapon against an enemy counter-attack was the sustained-fire Vickers.

The planners had to grapple with yet another major problem. Already, experience from the Somme told that the heavy loads carried by the attacking infantryman severely curtailed his ability to move and fight. The French in particular had begun to acknowledge the tactical flexibility and effectiveness of infantry who could move freely and quickly. With over thirty kilograms on their backs and a weapon and ammunition weighing a further ten, the infantryman's tactical flexibility was severely impaired. At Fromelles, the load included 150 rounds of ammunition, two hand grenades, two sandbags and two days' iron rations while every third man had a shovel or a pick to carry. This load made anything approaching rapid movement almost impossible.

The other side of the equation, however, was equally compelling. In a well-planned and prepared attack, the attacking infantry could usually capture sections of the enemy's trench. The problem then became one of consolidating and defending these until communication trenches could be dug from their own lines to connect with the captured trench and allow the passage of reinforcements. With the German artillery's well-practised ability to isolate successful attackers from their own lines, the materiel to consolidate and defend their gains had to be carried by the attackers themselves. It was not until the advent of the carrier tank some two years later that the first waves of attacking infantry were finally spared the necessity to carry with them sufficient supplies to sustain themselves for several days and permit some basic reconstruction of captured positions.

## The Plan of the Attack

The actual plan for the attack at Fromelles has been stridently condemned by some of those who took part and practically all those who have written about it since. There can be no doubt that the plan contained flaws and included some fundamental mistakes that the planners of the time should reasonably have been expected to avoid. How many of these errors were, however, a manifestation of the risk management approach to operational planning forced on the BEF by the strategic and logistic circumstances of the moment has yet to be determined. The first problem in assessing whether the outcome was the result of an error or an accident lies in identifying precisely the orders for the attack, who drafted which parts and the input of the various levels of command in their preparation. While ultimately it was the infantry who paid for these errors, they also made many mistakes of their own. In this battle, the inexperience and low standard of training of practically all those involved made the probability of failure very high.

Orders from higher commands rarely come as a surprise or involve unexpected tasking. Indeed, in this war, the usual process saw higher headquarters advising its immediate subordinate commanders of a requirement to conduct a specific operation in a specific area with specifically identified resources to achieve an identified and specific end. The subordinate commander would be tasked to develop a plan to achieve this. The higher headquarters would then analyse the plan and respond by altering either the supporting resources to be allocated or reducing the set objectives or, in many cases, overriding the plans and objections of the subordinate commander and issuing detailed orders of their own. Haig followed this process at the tactical and operational level of war, with Sir Henry Rawlinson, the Commander of Fourth Army, responsible for planning the Somme offensive.

As outlined earlier, the attack at Fromelles was based on a plan for a slightly different operation that was then modified to accommodate changed objectives and tactical developments. The final plan was a composition of the opinions and judgements of Haig's Deputy Chief of Staff, First Army Commander, Monro, the Corps Commander, Haking, the two divisional commanders plus all their specialist advisers. A plan such as this is not a monolithic document but includes several different component parts such as the artillery plan, the medical evacuation plan and the resupply plan, among others. The Army Commander's orders are part of the plan, and he sets broad objectives, broad timings and allocates specialist combat support. The Corps Commander then sets specific objectives and timings and allocates support according to his assessment of the difficulty faced by each attacking element. The divisional commanders and the brigade commanders do much the same, but on a smaller scale and with fewer resources. For example, each brigade commander was responsible for deciding which two of his four battalions would lead the assault and where his brigade support assets, the machine-gun company and the light trench mortar battery (if he had one), would focus their support. Even the smallest combat element, the infantry section, would make some plans for manoeuvre, identification, lines of approach to the objectives and timings — all based on the original overall concept of the attack.

A group of unidentified Australian soldiers building sandbag parapet trenches in a reserve line of a defence system.
AWM EZ0041

# Myths and Misconceptions

Among the many myths and misconceptions that continue to plague understanding of the Great War, the notion of the *chateau general* is one of the worst. The meaning of the term is vague and imprecise but seems intended to imply that the generals running the battles chose to stay or even hide from its realities in their luxurious accommodation far to the rear and, by implication, far from danger. The criticism seems to suggest that, had they been 'real men', they would have been in the front-line trenches with their soldiers, sharing the same hardships and dangers. And what value would they have provided if they had? One more soldier shooting at the Germans was hardly going to influence the outcome of the battle. A general's value lay in the way he could direct the battle by increasing effort in successful areas and halting it where failure was clear. To do this, he had to be in a place where communication could reach him, where he could spread and view maps of the entire battlefield and quickly access specialist advice from his artillerymen, airmen and logistics experts. He needed to know how many troops were available and where they were; he needed to know the state of ammunition and food for all his forces. He needed to know the state of his troops' morale. How could he do all this in a trench where communication was largely non-existent? Any activity such as this would have inevitably attracted the full might of German artillery, an outcome for which the front-line soldier would not have thanked his general.

The popular image conjured by the term is a fundamental misunderstanding of the way warfare was conducted. All the generals were well aware of conditions in the front line and on the battlefield. Even a cursory glance at the war diaries of the various headquarters reveals reams of reports on this very subject. Air reconnaissance was conducted daily and observers' reports and images went to the same headquarters the critics claim were ignorant of conditions. Headquarters sent officers forward on a daily basis to discuss operations and conditions while the generals themselves made regular visits to units under their command. The image of the out-of-touch sybarite simply does not stand up to analysis. Yet the worst aspect of this popular image is the implication that the generals were somehow cowardly for not exposing themselves to the same dangers as their troops and dissolute for living in comparative luxury. Leaving aside the proportionally large numbers who were killed and wounded during the war while in command, this accusation clearly fails to examine the personal record of the British High Command. Most had battle experience from previous wars and had acquitted themselves well, with many holding bravery awards. As for comfort, even Australia's popular favourite wartime commander, Lieutenant General Sir John Monash, had a reputation for enjoying a comfortable existence for most of the war. Why this is a problem is unclear. Do the critics believe the generals would have made better military decisions if they, too, had been wet, cold, hungry and frightened? It is unlikely their troops would have thought so — they would more likely have considered them mad.

One part of the plan that was severely criticised after the war was the insistence by some commanders that sally ports (specially reinforced covered exits built into the front of the breastworks) be used rather than have assault troops climb over the top of the breastworks. The consequence of this decision was that the troops had to move out of the shelter of the front trenches into No Man's Land quite early, as egress through these ports was painfully slow. Critics point to the significant number of casualties incurred amongst troops waiting in No Man's Land and to the confusion that accompanied this initial phase. They also point to the casualties caused by using the sally ports in the face of pre-registered enemy machine-gun fire. What alternatives were available to commanders?

German artillery was already causing heavy casualties in the advancing troops. Exposing them even more by having them climb over a high, wide and flat surface exposed to shrapnel and shell fragments and machine-gun fire already registered on the top of the breastwork line, would only have increased the casualty count. There were some concealed subterranean exits and why these were not used at all remains unclear. However, if the use of sally ports slowed the deployment, use of these exits may have clogged it completely. As they were not used, it is impossible to know whether the Germans had plotted their path and pre-registered the exits in the same way as they had the sally ports. Had they done so, the cost of using them would have been comparable to the losses actually experienced. At least while in the sally ports and within the minimal shelter of the shallow trenches in No Man's Land, the infantry had some protection. While no evidence has been found to support this conjecture, it is possible the commanders on the spot were willing to accept the limitations inherent in using the sally ports in return for fewer casualties during this particularly vulnerable part of the attack.

The final plan was not noticeably different to the standard plan common for offensive operations during the war. In terms of layout, methodology and terminology, it was a standard operational order. First Army Operational Order No. 100 to Commander XI Corps specified timings, objectives, which division would attack the different objectives, and set out coordination and timings, such as when the guns would fire at the front line and when they would adjust fire to other areas.

## The Artillery Plan

A critical part of any attack in this war was the artillery fire plan. Devised almost without reference to the attacking infantry, who were expected to conform to the timings of the gunners, effective artillery was critical to any attack's chance of success. The senior gunners, particularly at divisional and corps level, were major participants in any operational planning. Their views, and frequently the views of the divisional commanders, were sought while the plan was being developed. There were several senior planning conferences held during the lead-up to Fromelles, evidence that the popular view that the plan was a single-handed creation is incorrect. In the five days leading up to the attack, conferences were held every day and occasionally more frequently. They were held at First Army, corps and divisional headquarters. Some of the conferences involved just the commanders, others just the specialists — there were two artillery conferences — but most included all the relevant command and planning staffs.

The success or failure of the overall attack would be determined by the success or failure of the artillery. Artillery had two roles in the early stages of an attack: the first to destroy obstacles such as the barbed-wire belts protecting the enemy's trenches, and strong points or machine-gun nests; the second to suppress the enemy's defensive fire. Once the attack was under way, the artillery's role was to cut the enemy's forward trenches from his reserve area, to counter the enemy's artillery to stop it firing on the attacking troops, and lay down a curtain of shellfire, called a box barrage, around the captured objective until the infantry was able to consolidate it sufficiently to resist an enemy counter-attack. The guns were also expected to break up enemy counter-attack forces assembling in his rear area. As the various orders issued for this battle indicate, both Monro and Haking understood perfectly the artillery role and its contribution to eventual success. It is also clear that they understood the risks involved in relying on partially trained artillerymen.

These two facts placed the commanders in a quandary. The plan depended on the gunners undertaking complex artillery tasks; but the gunners available were unlikely to achieve these. This problem lies at the heart of current criticisms of the battle. The problem confronting both Monro and Haking was, in view of the known limitations of the artillery, whether these limitations were sufficient to justify the cancellation of the attack. There was plenty of evidence pointing to the problems faced even by competent gunners on the Somme in meeting their objectives. Yet any concern was offset by new solutions for overcoming these which were introduced even as the Somme battle was raging. On 16 July, a memo was released by GHQ, Order O.A. 256, outlining a more effective method for infantry to advance under cover of artillery fire. In the context of the Fromelles attack and the fact that it had been initiated by the High Command, abandoning the attack simply on the grounds that the artillery might fail would have been a difficult decision to make.

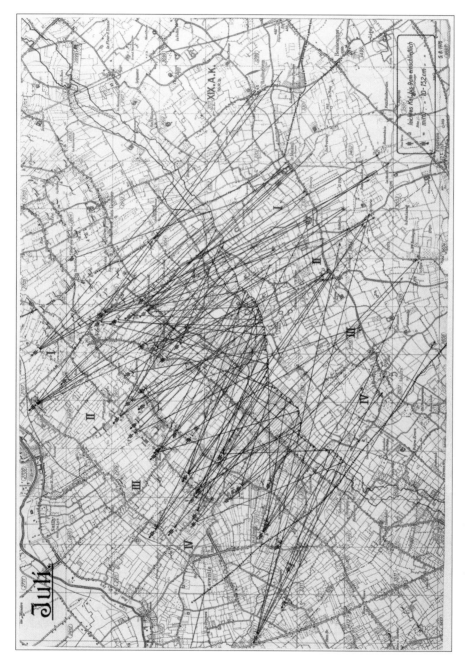

German map showing plotted location of British artillery firing during the battle. Map supplied as part of a report by Peter Barton on his research on behalf of the Australian Army in the *Hauptstaatsarchiv Kriegsarchiv* in Munich, Germany.

# Ordnance QF 18-pdr Gun

| | |
|---|---|
| **Calibre:** | 83.8mm (3.3in) |
| **Weight:** | 1284kg |
| **Crew**: | Six |
| **Rate of Fire:** | 20rpm (max); 4rpm (sustained) |
| **Effective Range**: | 6000m max (in 1916) |
| **Manufacturer:** | British arsenals and in Allied countries under licence |

Accepted for service by the British Army in 1904, the QF (Quick Firing) 18-pdr was the standard field gun of all Commonwealth armies in World War One with almost 300 shipped to Australia in 1906 for use by the various militia artillery units. While the gun had been improved by 1916, it proved inadequate for the primary role of artillery on the Western Front — the destruction of fortifications, trench-lines and barbed wire. Firing mainly shrapnel shells on a relatively flat trajectory, the 18-pdr's shells had little penetrating power. Even by the Battle of Fromelles, when the shortage of high explosive ammunition had been addressed, the 18-pdr remained relatively ineffective against all but enemy troops in the open, witnessing the rise of larger and heavier calibre guns. Towed by a limber containing twenty-four rounds of ammunition and team of six or eight horses, the gun was usually dug in when deployed on the Western Front. The 18-pdr field gun's comparatively short (by modern standards) range necessitated its location as far forward as possible in order to extend its reach into the enemy's rear areas. Smaller calibre guns were located between 900 and 2,700 metres from the front line, while the heavier calibre guns were located further to the rear. This meant that the guns were often located immediately behind the forward battalions, a practice not without its hazards. At the battle of Lagnicourt in April 1917, the guns from all four batteries of the 2nd Australian Field Artillery (AFA) Brigade, together with the three field batteries of the 1st AFA Brigade, were captured in a German counter-attack.

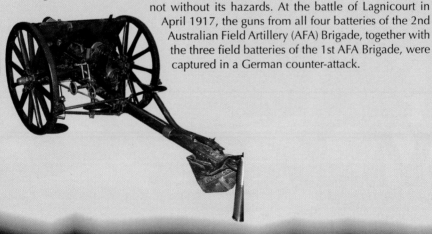

*Above:* A battery of field guns in action: in this case the 14th battery, AFA, in action during the Passchendaele attack in 1917. AWME00920

*Below*: Close-up of the breech of an 18-pdr field gun. (Photo courtesy of Major John Gallagher and the Australian Army Artillery Museum, Sydney)

The artillery assembled for the attack was, despite some claims to the contrary, numerically sufficient. With one gun for every eight metres of enemy front trench, the ratio was similar to that for the successful 14 July attack on the Somme. In addition to the two attacking divisions' own artillery resources, Haking was provided with significant artillery reinforcements. The final number of guns represented a denser ratio of gun to objective than was available for the first day on the Somme.

# Ordnance QF 4.5-inch Howitzer

| | |
|---|---|
| **Calibre:** | 114mm (4.5in) |
| **Weight:** | 1370kg |
| **Crew**: | Ten |
| **Rate of Fire:** | 4rpm |
| **Effective Range**: | 6680m max (in 1916) |
| **Manufacturer:** | Coventry Ordnance Works & Ordnance Factory, Woolwich |

Introduced in 1909, the Ordnance QF (quick firing) 4.5-in howitzer was a horse-drawn field howitzer designed to be towed behind a limber and six horses. It presented an evolution in gun design that incorporated many of the lessons learnt during the Boer War. The 4.5-in howitzer was the standard British Empire field howitzer of World War One. In 1916, field artillery brigades were being issued one battery of 4.5-in howitzers for three batteries of 18-pdrs. However, by the Battle of Fromelles, a number of divisions retained an artillery brigade of three 4.5-in howitzer batteries (each of six guns). Its calibre (114mm) and hence shell weight were greater than those of the equivalent German field howitzer (105mm). Over 3,200 guns were produced by the end of the war, with Australian batteries deploying to the Western Desert in the Second World War still equipped with 4.5-in howitzers. These were replaced by the new 25-pdr in 1940.

*Above*: A good study of a 4.5-inch howitzer in action. This picture is of a gun still in service and being used on a range west of Ipswich in Queensland in 1938 or 1939.
AWM P01485_014

*Right*: Close-up of the breech of a 4.5-inch howitzer. (Photo courtesy of Major John Gallagher and the Australian Army Artillery Museum, Sydney)

## Artillery Support for the Attack

| Artillery type | Gun type | Number of Guns |
|---|---|---|
| Heavy and siege artillery | | |
| | 60-pounder | 40 |
| | 6-inch howitzer | 22 |
| | 9.2-inch howitzer | 8 |
| | 12-inch howitzer | 5 |
| | 6-inch gun | 2 |
| | 9.2-inch gun | 1 |
| Field artillery | | |
| | 18-pounder guns | 232 |
| | 4.5-inch howitzer | 64 |

*Source:* compiled from war diaries and Official Histories.

The fire plan developed to support the attack was a straightforward concept designed to suppress the enemy during the advance and assault phase and protect friendly troops during the consolidation phase. Adding to the mixed message concerning secrecy, the plan also included an initial deception plan — the day before the attack, enemy trenches seven miles south of the objective were to be bombarded to entice the enemy into moving his artillery south to meet the threat. The barrage was to continue on the morning of the attack, enabling the guns supporting the infantry to register the range without attracting undue attention.

Commencing on 14 July and continuing despite days of indecision over the future of the attack, the artillery maintained a regular if desultory fire on the enemy's trenches and approaches. The bad weather made engaging targets on and beyond Aubers Ridge difficult, as air observation was impossible. On the day before, clearing weather allowed aircraft from Nos. 10 and 16 Squadrons, RFC, and observation balloons from No. 10 Kite Balloon Section to recommence spotting for the guns. On the day itself, morning haze delayed the artillery barrage which, in turn, forced a postponement of the infantry attack. The guns required a specific period of time to complete the final preparatory tasks of cutting the enemy's barbed-wire defences and strong points.

Artillery observers reported to headquarters during each phase of the artillery preparation and the XI Corps headquarters war diaries reveal that all the observers reported that the artillery was doing its job well. The watching infantry were of the same opinion, although the number of their own shells falling on them tempered their admiration for the gunners' efforts. A special bombardment of the Sugarloaf salient by the heavy artillery was timed to begin at 2.35 pm. There is no suggestion in the reports of the observers before the infantry assault began that there were any concerns about artillery failure. Reports from patrols in No Man's Land during the preceding night that highlighted areas of uncut wire were addressed by special variations in the fire plan timetable to allow those areas to be re-targeted. On all the evidence available to the commanders on the spot, the guns had fully prepared the position: there were no grounds for calling off the infantry attack.

Balloon busting.
(Jeff Isaacs)

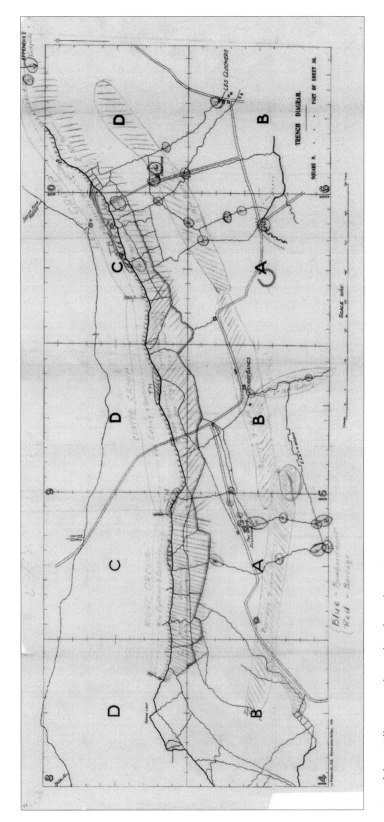

Part of the Artillery Fire Plan, taken from the XI Corps War Diary.

## The Infantry Plan

The infantry plan, as set out in XI Corps Order 100, was straightforward. Two companies from each of the six brigades of the two divisions would move into No Man's Land at times that were fixed depending on the distance to be covered, form up into attack waves and position themselves as close as possible to the enemy's front trenches. At 6.00 pm, the barrage would lift from the enemy's front trenches — the signal for the infantry to assault the positions. Having taken the front trench system, the assault was to continue to capture the support-line trenches. The depth of penetration of the enemy's line was determined by the depth of these support trenches but at no point was the penetration to be more than a few hundred metres. Initial plans to capture some particularly troublesome enemy strong points further to the rear, such as Delangré Farm, were cancelled. The plan estimated that using the three brigades side by side would generate sufficient combat power to capture such a limited objective. Based on experience from the Somme and Verdun, this was not an unrealistic expectation, provided the artillery destroyed the enemy defences and suppressed the defenders further away from the point of attack.

Once in the enemy front lines, the attackers were to despatch bombing parties laterally along the trench system to link up with flanking assaulting units. On the left and right flank of the operation, successive waves of attackers were tasked with establishing blocks and strong points to protect their vulnerable flanks. While the attack was still under way, successive waves of infantry from the remaining battalions of the brigades would carry forward stores of all types, reinforce the captured positions and expand the captured area. Parties of engineers, pioneers and other infantry would dig communication trenches and saps from the attackers' front lines to provide a more protected means of moving to the captured trenches. A movement plan was developed to ensure the forward movement of men and stores was not interrupted by returning working parties or the evacuation of wounded or prisoners of war.

The only area of potential confusion was the inter-divisional boundary. The left battalion of the 61st Division and the right battalion of the 5th Australian Division had to attack on converging lines as the front curved around the Sugarloaf feature. The Sugarloaf itself was the objective of the 61st and the Australians were tasked with seizing the length of trench immediately behind it. The potential risk of each side firing on the other was covered in the assault plan.

Despite the controversy surrounding the battle, there is nothing in either the artillery plan or the infantry plan which differs markedly from similar plans for other (successful) attacks. The same elements are addressed: timings, objectives, support, lines of demarcation, reporting requirements and methods of communication. As the battle was to demonstrate, while there were substantial failures in many of the assumptions underlying the plans, the plans themselves conformed to the military standards of the day.

Fleurbaix, France 1916, soldiers walk along a path beside a row of front-line trenches.
AWM P00437.017

# CHAPTER FIVE

# THE ATTACK

Oblique of Fromelles area from the air showing Australian and German lines. AWM E05990

## Preparations

The haste with which the planning was completed and the forces involved assembled led to much confusion and generated many problems. Both divisions earmarked for the attack were in the front line when the decision to use them was made. For the men of the 61st, who already occupied their designated attacking position, there would be little rest and even less time to train for the attack. The Australian division was not in position and had to hand over its section of the line, retire to the communication zone and move forward into its attack areas on the day of the attack. Half the Australians had not seen their front line objectives at all.

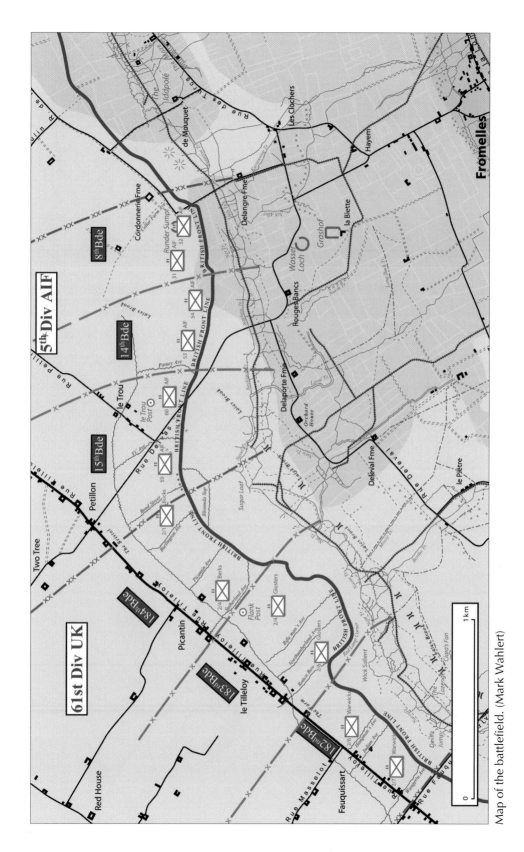

Map of the battlefield. (Mark Wahlert)

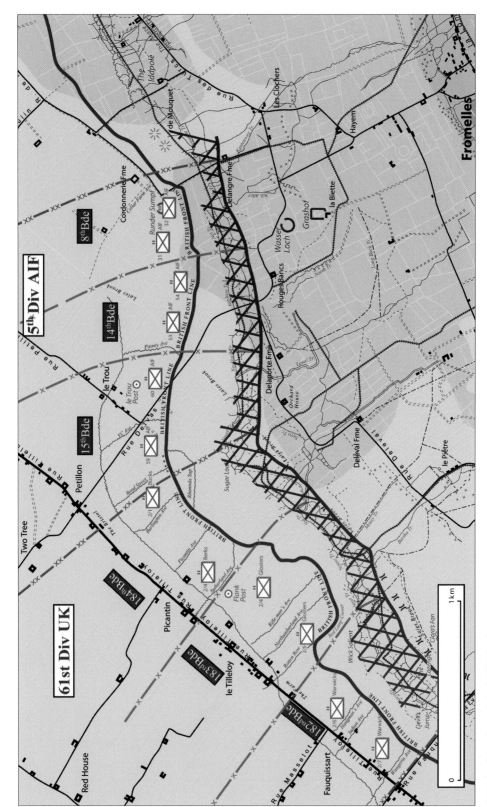

British objectives. (Mark Wahlert)

# Ordnance BL 8-in Howitzer Mk V

| | |
|---|---|
| **Calibre:** | 203mm (8 inches) |
| **Weight:** | 14 tonnes |
| **Crew**: | eight |
| **Rate of Fire:** | 2rpm |
| **Effective Range**: | 9600m (max for Mk V) |

The early British 8-in howitzer (Mk I to V) was a British improvisation developed early in World War One to provide heavy artillery. It used shortened and bored-out barrels from various redundant naval 6-in guns and bore no relation to later 8-in howitzers in World War One (such as the Vickers 8-in Mark VI to VIII howitzers). The early 8-in howitzer was initially operated by siege batteries of the Royal Garrison Artillery (RGA) and introduced to destroy enemy trenches and fortifications. The Mk V proved difficult to manoeuvre on the battlefield due to its overall weight of 14 tonnes. It was also difficult to supply, with each round weighing 91 kg. The improvised nature of the design led to problems such as premature explosion and unreliability in action, and the field workshops found the guns difficult to maintain. There were also early quality control problems with British mass production of ammunition in 1915 and early 1916: 'the 8-inch fuses failed so often that the battlefield was littered with unexploded 8-inch shells'. By the Battle of the Somme in mid-1916, some of these problems had been corrected — 'They were monstrous things and extremely heavy, but the machinery of the guns was very simple.' They remained in use on the Western Front throughout World War One as Britain's need for heavy artillery increased and was never fully met by the production of modern equipment.

## Moving Forward

To the south-west, and on the right half of the attack, the troops of the 61st Division began to move into No Man's Land under the protection of the artillery barrage. The use of the barrage as a form of protection in an attack was increasingly understood by even the junior leaders of infantry sections. They knew that, for an attack to succeed, the assaulting troops had to be as close to the enemy line as possible when the barrage lifted. Encouraged by this knowledge, junior leaders pushed as far forward as they could, accepting casualties from their own artillery if necessary. But, for the 61st, this tactic was to prove only partially successful.

## 182nd Brigade

On the extreme right, the 182nd Brigade began the attack with two battalions side by side: the 2/7th Battalion of the Royal Warwickshire Regiment — known as the Warwicks — on the right and the 2/6th Warwicks to their left. Due to the relatively effective British artillery preparation in this sector, German artillery and *minenwerfer* fire had not succeeded in breaking up the attacking formations of the right-hand battalion as they had elsewhere along the assault line. Consequently, the two assault companies, C and D, left their trenches at 5.30 pm in relatively good order and

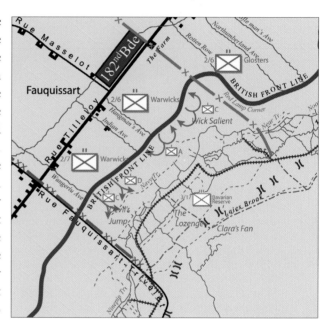

182nd Brigade initial phase.
(Mark Wahlert)

advanced to within fifty metres of the enemy breastworks by the time the barrage lifted at 6.00 pm.

The 2/6th Warwicks were not as fortunate. Prior to the attack, casualties from German artillery had been remarkably low — just eight, according to the unit war diary. This changed as the assault companies, A and C, left their trenches at 5.31 pm. German artillery fire hit the left-hand end of the line, killing or wounding many — including all the officers — and disorganising the assault formation. The Warwicks had been given a particularly difficult assignment, as the section of enemy trench they had to capture included another strong defensive salient — the Wick salient. While not as strong nor as well sited as the Sugarloaf, it remained a formidable obstacle. Despite the presence of the strong point and the heavy casualties inflicted by the German artillery, the two companies of the Warwicks continued to push forward until, when the barrage lifted, they were within eighty metres of the Wick salient itself.

## 183rd Brigade

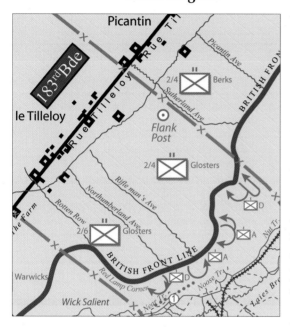

183rd Brigade initial phase.
(Mark Wahlert)

The next brigade along, the 183rd, enjoyed a singular advantage. No Man's Land to its front was the narrowest on the entire divisional attack front — between 150 and 200 metres wide. This shorter distance significantly reduced the time the assault troops were exposed on open ground. Unfortunately, it also meant that the enemy was closer and thus able to maximise the effectiveness of small arms fire during the early and crucial forming-up period outside the cover of the breastworks. Engineering work prior to the assault provided some additional cover, further reducing the 183rd's exposure time. At 4.30 pm, prior to the troops' departure from the line, engineers had exploded some 'pipe-pusher' charges to create instant shallow trenches linking the assault trenches with the immediate objective.

Unfortunately, this sound preparation was negated by excellent German artillery fire which so depleted the two assault battalions, the 2/6th Battalion of the Royal Gloucestershire Regiment (the Glosters) on the right and the 2/4th Glosters on the left, that they had to call up their reserve companies immediately. German machine-gun fire on the sally port exits also slowed and disrupted the move into No Man's Land. The report of the Commanding Officer of the 2/4th Glosters clearly indicates that the problem lay not so much in the use of the sally ports as the existence of a large number of unsuppressed German machine-guns at close range with a good view of the available approach paths. The German commander in this sector had, unusually, ordered his sentries to remain at their lookout positions during the British barrage and was thus warned the moment the first assault troops entered No Man's Land. While this is some indication of the courage of the Bavarian defenders, it is also an indictment of the British barrage of this part of the line as no enemy should have been able to remain in the open and survive.

The two assault companies of the 2/6th Glosters entered the sally ports at 5.40 pm, some nine minutes after the 2/4th. This delay gave the watching Germans time to train machine-gun fire on the exits. The dead, the wounded and the disoriented effectively blocked the exits for most of the assaulting companies. The third and fourth waves had no option but to exit over the breastworks and were almost destroyed by machine-gun fire and shrapnel. Somehow, a small number of the 2/6th was able to assemble in No Man's Land and move close to the enemy line by the 6.00 pm lifting of the barrage.

The 2/4th Glosters initially fared better than its sister battalion. After entering the sally ports at 5.31 pm,

## Pipe-pushers

Pipe-pushers were lengths of steel pipe filled with explosive — usually ammonal — that were pushed through the sub-surface soil by mechanical means for considerable distances. Because of the method used to deploy them, they had to be installed from within the shelter of a friendly trench, which limited their ability to reach the enemy lines. Once blown they produced a straight but shallow temporary trench usually around 3 – 4 ft (called a 'sap') that provided the assaulting troops some protection from shellfire and enemy machine-gun and small arms fire from their flanks. The presence of the pipe-pushing device in the front trench was difficult to conceal and inevitably and quickly brought heavy enemy artillery fire onto the position.

one company, A Company, moved three platoons into No Man's Land and formed up for the attack. The other assault company, D Company, pushed one platoon through before the Germans opened heavy machine-gun fire on the exits and the deployed troops in the open. The leading platoon was driven back into the sally ports and no further exit was possible. The German fire then moved onto A Company and, by 6.10 pm, had driven the three platoons already in No Man's Land back to the ports. In the face of heavy, accurate and sustained machine-gun fire, no further advance by the 2/4th Glosters was possible.

## 184th Brigade

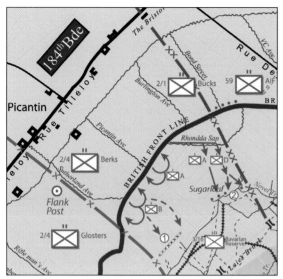

184th Brigade initial phase.
(Mark Wahlert)

The last of the British brigades in the attack, the 184th, shared the divisional boundary with the Australian 15th Brigade to its left. The 184th Brigade also opted for the classic two-battalion-wide attack, with the 2/4th Battalion of the Royal Berkshire Regiment (the Berks) on the right and the 2/1st Bucks (part of the Oxfordshire and Buckinghamshire Light Infantry Regiment) on the left with the Australian 59th Battalion to its left. The British and Australian brigades shared a boundary but, given that they were to advance on converging paths, a V-shaped wedge — filled by a section of machine-guns from the 15th Brigade — had been formed with its apex on the Sugarloaf feature and its base on the British line.

The 184th Brigade faced the formidable task of attacking the Sugarloaf salient itself. The Sugarloaf had been subject to several intensive but largely ineffective barrages by British artillery. Once again, the massive and rapid expansion of the artillery arm, which meant that the gunners were inexperienced and their equipment still unreliable, was to have severe consequences for the infantrymen. The German defenders of the salient remained free to enfilade any attacking waves approaching the first German defensive line with machine-gun fire. The failure of the artillery to destroy, or even temporarily neutralise this position was one of the main contributing factors to both the failure of the attack and the high casualty count. This was doubly so given that No Man's Land in front of the 184th was over 400 metres wide with little or no cover, especially on the flanks.

Even before the move into No Man's Land, both battalions suffered heavy casualties from accurate and intense German artillery fire. Like the Australians next to them, both battalions were densely packed in their forward trenches waiting for the signal to move forward. Clearly visible to German artillery observers, they made inviting targets. The 2/4th Berks incurred over forty casualties while the 2/1st Bucks suffered over 100. This forced the call-up of the reserve companies and the inevitable confusion and ad hoc restructuring of the tactical attack plan.

123

At 5.40 pm A and B Companies, the two assault companies of the 2/4th Berks, exited from their sally ports under the watchful gaze of the Germans. Their task was to capture and isolate the trenches immediately to the south-west of the Sugarloaf salient. These trenches were defended by *12 Company, 3/16th Bavarian Reserve Infantry Regiment* whose young commander, when informed of the attack, immediately ordered his troops to man their machine-guns. Without the protection of an effective barrage to force the defenders to take cover, every attempt by the assault troops in No Man's Land to form up for the attack was defeated by concentrated machine-gun and small arms fire. The confusion caused by casualties and heavy losses among officers and NCOs drove many of the survivors of the first waves back to their own trenches, disrupting the forward movement of successive waves. Some attempted to climb back over the parapets but usually met the same fate as those who had tried to advance by the same route. Those who advanced towards the enemy line found the barbed-wire defences uncut. (Point 1 in map.) These were mainly leaderless survivors of B Company who were quickly forced back by enemy fire delivered from almost point-blank range. When the barrage lifted at 6.00 pm, there were no troops from the 2/4th left to begin the attack.

The 2/1st Bucks had drawn the unenviable task of capturing the Sugarloaf itself. Not only was it the farthest objective from the jumping-off point, it was such an obvious target that its defenders had carefully prepared defensive plans to protect it. A full-scale frontal attack over open ground was always going to be difficult without effective support and careful initial preparation. Unhappily for the 2/1st, the artillery preparation had been ineffective, counter-battery fire to suppress German artillery was still not a well-understood technique and there was no attempt to protect the advance by concealing it with smoke, even though smoke candles had been made available (ironically, smoke from the battle itself later added to the confusion and breakdown in command for the British and Australian commanders). The distance from friendly trenches also made mining and similar offensive techniques used in the 5th Division sector difficult to employ here.

One feature, a two-metre-deep trench known as the Rhondda Sap, snaked its way across No Man's Land and provided some protection to the assaulting troops. Attempts in the early afternoon by the Australian 3rd Tunnelling Company to improve the Rhondda Sap and its approaches to the enemy's line were spotted by the Germans and attracted heavy artillery fire (the tunnelling companies were corps and army troops used for special tasks and occasionally employed to provide specialist support for specific operations. These Australians were not part of the 5th Division).

# 77mm Field Gun *Feldkanone* M.96

| | |
|---|---|
| **Calibre:** | 77mm (3.03in) |
| **Weight:** | 925kg |
| **Crew**: | six |
| **Rate of Fire:** | 5rpm |
| **Effective Range**: | 11000m (max in 1916) |
| **Manufacturer:** | Krupp Corporation |

The German 77mm M96 was the most common field gun in the German Army at the outbreak of World War One. Upgraded and improved as the war progressed, by 1916 its accuracy and range had increased, although it remained inferior to its French rival (the Canon 75mm) in rate of fire. A key advantage of this gun was the ability to manoeuvre it around the battlefield. It was relatively light for a gun of that time and could be manhandled by its crew and quickly repositioned. This was important to the German Army early in the war as it planned to out-manoeuvre and overrun all opposition. However, as the battlefield bogged down into static trench warfare, its mobility was no longer a key advantage. During the Battle of Fromelles, the 77mm *Feldkanone* was one of the most numerous guns facing the Australians. However, it lacked the punch of the British QF 18-pdr. The 77 was commonly known to Allied troops as a 'whizz-bang', due to its high velocity — the 'whizz' of the arriving shell and the 'bang' of its detonation were almost simultaneous.

German 77mm Field Gun M96.
(Courtesy of the Department of Veterans' Affairs)

A and D Companies, the two assault companies from the 2/1st Bucks, had occupied their jumping-off trenches since nine o'clock that morning and had already incurred heavy casualties from accurate enemy artillery fire. A Company was still recovering from the loss of seventy-eight men the previous day when a British 'drop-short'(the troops' nickname for one of their own shells falling short) had exploded a poison gas cylinder in their midst. While the company had been reinforced, it remained under strength despite the fact that it faced the most challenging tasks of any of the assaulting troops. Although between them the two companies could muster only 120 men, they were tasked with occupying a frontage of 400 metres and crossing almost 450 metres of open ground.

At 5.40 pm, both companies moved into No Man's Land in preparation for the attack. With the German machine-gunners focused on their sally ports, both companies used the Rhondda Sap to move men out into No Man's Land ready for the assault when the barrage lifted. This move was partially successful, so that by 5.40, enough troops had made it along the sap to a form four, very under strength assault waves. Without the protection of the sap, the 2/1st would almost certainly have been stopped at the sally ports.

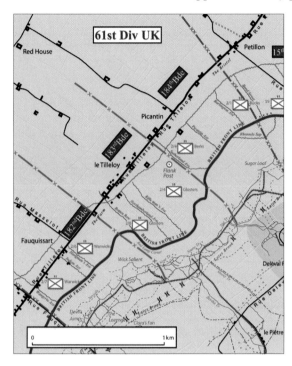

The divisional boundary between both attacking divisions intersects the Sugarloaf feature. (Mark Wahlert)

In view of the obvious tactical importance of the Sugarloaf position, arranging the attack with the Sugarloaf salient on the junction of the two attacking forces was not tactically ideal. Apart from the issues discussed earlier, the tactical cooperation and coordination necessary between all the assaulting troops was made immeasurably more complicated by having two entirely separate commands responsible for the two halves of the operation. The need for a single command responsible for the attack on the feature was even more important given the complex manoeuvring required of the assaulting troops. Starting with a gap of almost 300 metres between them, the two attacking forces were to advance on converging lines. Under these circumstances, coordination was clearly a high priority to ensure mutual support and avoid incidents where friend fired on friend, known today as 'blue on blue' incidents. Such a situation did not arise as neither side could make the advances required, but, had either side been successful in its advance, the potential for friendly casualties was very real. This division of responsibility was to generate much post-war criticism of the entire plan, especially by the commander of the next brigade along the front, Brigadier General Harold (Pompey) Elliott. In this case, the criticism was warranted as communication breakdowns between the two brigades were a factor in the casualties suffered by Elliott's own 15th Brigade.

In an attempt to cover this vulnerable junction, the 5th Division stationed four Vickers machine-guns from the 15th Brigade Machine Gun Company and five Lewis guns from the 58th Battalion on the parapet to the right of the brigade. Their task was to neutralise the Sugarloaf until the advancing friendly troops masked the line of fire.

127

# Liaison

In warfare on the scale fought on the Western Front, one of the biggest problems, at all levels of command, was visibility of the situation in the sectors on either side of the commander's own formation. Problems with communication, language problems, different training and doctrinal methods (not an uncommon problem in coalition warfare) and the sheer scale of activity all combined to conceal from the commander what his neighbours were doing. This was an even greater problem where the boundary coincided with a divisional, corps, army or, in some cases, other army formation where the traditional 'chain of command' required communication to go up to the next headquarters rather than straight to the neighbouring unit. Numerous solutions were attempted, which is one reason the records of this period of the war are so full of memoranda on how other armies, corps etc. operated. By far the most effective solution was found to lie in the use of liaison officers. Liaison officers were sent from adjoining units to the headquarters of neighbouring formations for the express purpose of informing their own and other headquarters of plans, intentions and methods etc. They also advised the commander and staff of the intentions of their opposite number. Liaison officers were of differing ranks depending on the headquarters they represented and the one to which they were attached. They could range in rank from lieutenant to general and were often fluent in the language of the other headquarters. Even within established formations such as an Australian division, liaison officers from adjoining brigades were often attached to provide 'instant communication' between the two brigadier generals.

## 15th Australian Brigade

Along with the other brigade assault battalions, the two from the 15th Brigade, the 59th and 60th Battalions, had already been subjected to heavy artillery fire as they approached the front line. As they moved up in the early afternoon of 19 June, their progress was clearly visible to German artillery spotters both on Aubers Ridge and in observation balloons. The two 15th Brigade battalions suffered fewer casualties than the other two brigades and were fortunate also that the width of No Man's Land in front of them — some 400 metres — spared them the impact of the 'drop shorts' that plagued their fellow brigades. The narrower width of No Man's Land opposite both the 14th and 8th Brigades presented more of a challenge to accurate shooting for the inexperienced Australian gunners and the infantry suffered many unnecessary casualties through the errors they made.

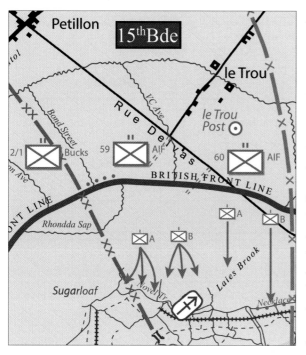

15th Brigade initial phase.
(Mark Wahlert)

Although the 59th and 60th Battalions managed to reach the limited protection of the forward trenches by 3.45 pm, they still had some two hours of waiting to endure before the attack was to begin. The densely packed mass of troops continued to provide an excellent target for German artillery and mortars and it was probably only due to the excess of targets available that more casualties were not incurred during this period of waiting. At 5.45 pm, the first wave from the two battalions moved out into No Man's Land with the 59th to the right, closest to the Sugarloaf and the 60th next to it (given the different widths of No Man's Land, start times had been staggered between the three brigades to allow all the assault troops to close with the enemy front line just as the barrage lifted). The second wave followed five minutes later. During these few minutes, the British barrage was mostly successful in keeping the German defenders in their shelters, with only sporadic rifle fire greeting the first waves. But the combination of distance and obstacles saw the lines of assaulting infantry still moving in the open when the barrage lifted to the enemy's rear positions at 6.02 pm.

## 14th Australian Brigade

To the left of the 15th Brigade, the 14th Brigade had tasked the 53rd Battalion (A and B Companies) and the 54th Battalion (also A and B Companies) with mounting the assault. The 53rd was positioned on the right, in touch with the 60th Battalion, with the 54th to its left. No Man's Land in front of the brigade varied in width from just under 100 metres in front of the 54th to almost 250 metres in front of the 53rd. The 54th Battalion had fared worst from the ongoing German artillery fire and inaccurate Australian shells, losing over fifty men, including three of its four company commanders and their seconds-in-command. Between them, the two leading assault waves had already lost over sixty men before leaving the forward 129 trenches at 5.43 pm. The enemy artillery also complicated the problems of moving the assaulting troops forward by blowing in the essential communication trenches or blocking them with debris. On the right of the brigade, A Company of the 53rd was immediately enfiladed by fire when it emerged from the sally ports. The machine-gun fire came not only from the front; the most damaging fire originated in that part of the enemy line that the 60th Battalion, on A Company's right, was supposed to have suppressed. While the whole of the 14th Brigade's line of advance was exposed by the 15th Brigade's inability to push forward, the remaining assaulting companies managed to cross No Man's Land relatively unscathed and form up for the assault in front of the enemy's parapets.

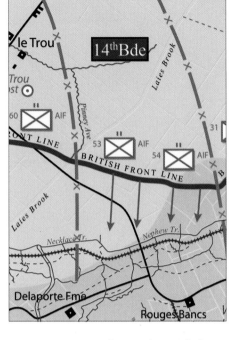

14th Brigade initial phase.
(Mark Wahlert)

## 8th Australian Brigade

The final sector was occupied by the 8th Brigade. This brigade had suffered severely from artillery fire, both friendly and enemy. The close proximity of the German lines worked against the inexperienced Australian gunners who lacked the skill to hit a target close to friendly troops. German artillery was more successful in its attack on the 8th Brigade's forward trenches than elsewhere and, apart from inflicting enormous casualties, also destroyed the 31st Battalion's ammunition dump. In its position on the flank, the 8th Brigade also came under fire from enemy batteries to the north, which meant that the concentration of fire was particularly heavy. By the time the advance was due to begin, the toll of casualties had forced the 8th Brigade Commander to combine the third and fourth waves into one, severely reducing the strength and combat power of the follow-on waves.

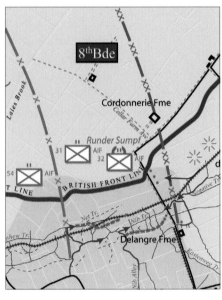

8th Brigade initial phase.
(Mark Wahlert)

The two assaulting battalions of the 8th Brigade, the 31st Battalion on the right and the 32nd on the left, had the shortest distance to advance of any of the Australian assault troops. This meant that they could delay their move into No Man's Land until the last moment. The first wave left its trenches at

5.53 pm while the second wave left only as the barrage lifted from the enemy's front line at six o'clock. At first, the defenders caused significant losses as the attacking troops crossed the 100 metres of No Man's Land, the enemy's efforts aided by enfilade fire from further north-east. In spite of the losses and the intensity of the defenders' fire, both battalions' leading waves were close to the enemy breastworks when the barrage lifted.

The planners had recognised the tactically difficult position of the left-hand battalion in this assault and made some specific provisions to protect the exposed left flank of the entire assault line. The shape of the front line, which turned more north-east on the divisional boundary line, meant that the moment the assault troops left their front trenches, they would be exposed to enfilade fire from the front and rear of their flank. Two schemes were devised to neutralise enemy fire on the assault troops. The 60th British Brigade, on the 8th Brigade's left, was to engage the enemy trenches to its front with small arms fire during the assault phase. A plan to release poisonous gas from the 60th line failed because the wind was blowing from the wrong direction. Finally, at six o'clock as the attack began, a large mine was detonated in No Man's Land just east of the approach path of the 32nd Battalion. Unfortunately for the 8th Brigade, the Bavarian defenders exhibited great bravery and determination and quickly recovered, continuing to fire into the flank of the advancing Australians.

## Summary

It was clear from this manoeuvre phase that all was not well, although both ends of the assault line had been able to move close enough to their initial objectives to be well placed to launch their attacks. The closer each divisional assault element was to the central point of the assault line — the Sugarloaf feature — the less distance the advance achieved. For the 184th Brigade, this problem was compounded by the presence on the right flank of the still functioning Wick salient. The attack had yet to begin in earnest and already the causes of its ultimate failure were present. The failure of the artillery to destroy or neutralise the enemy's strong points, artillery and mortars, the failure of the intelligence system to locate and pinpoint the enemy's artillery for counter-battery fire and, in particular, the failure of the artillery to cut the bulk of the enemy's defensive barbed-wire belts were the primary causes of the difficulties at this early stage in the attack.

The real problem, however, was communication. Did the commanders know of the problems in the critical lead-up phase and, if so, what could they do about them? This battle clearly highlights the Achilles heel of all military operations at the time — communication. It is clear from the war diaries that at even the lowest formation-level headquarters closest to the assaulting troops, and even in this first phase of the attack, no clear picture existed of what was happening and what could be done to correct failures. All headquarters war diaries are replete with reports from artillery observers informing them that the artillery fire was satisfactory and that progress by the assaulting troops was good.

In the opening stages, when reports were received such as those indicating that the bombardment of the Sugarloaf had not suppressed defending fire, command responded quickly and positively by ordering more artillery fire onto the feature. Artillery fire could be adjusted to revisit areas that had not been damaged sufficiently by the initial barrage — but this could not occur once the infantry had gone forward. Timely communication was also seriously degraded by the destruction of the phone network as telephone lines and exchanges were destroyed. The lack of reliable communication with the forward troops meant commanders could not take the risk of deviating from the agreed original fire plan for fear of hitting troops who may have moved into the target area. The troops manoeuvring to assault the enemy line had no option but to move forward in accordance with the original plan and their commanders could do little to provide additional support once the battle had begun.

The Signal Office and Headquarters of the 4th Australian Divisional Signalling Company situated on the outskirts of Vaulx on the Vaulx-Beugny Road. A motorcyclist despatch rider is seen leaving for the forward units with a basket containing carrier pigeons for distribution among the fighting troops. AWM E00647

# Communication

The exercise of command and control over troops once the battle had commenced was an ongoing problem that remained unresolved in this war. Poor and unreliable communication was the major contributor to this problem. Until the advent of massed armies and weapons with a long-range capability, the commander had been able to survey the whole battlefield from his horse or a convenient hilltop. He could use flags, signal lights, even trumpets and drums or mounted messengers to take tactical orders to wherever required. The commander knew what was happening as it was happening and could intervene, often decisively, to correct a problem. He could order forward reinforcements, stop or extend an advance or provide additional support from his reserves. All this command flexibility came to a halt when armies and the battlefield grew too large, the battlefield became too dangerous and the battle too fast for this old method to continue to operate. Unfortunately for the commander of the day, the need for better, faster and more reliable two-way communication remained largely beyond the technology of the time. Communication is a simple word for a complex military problem. In the military context of the war, the difficulty of communicating became worse closer to the front line. In the rear areas, telephones provided a comparatively secure, high volume method for transmitting and receiving information. Telephone was also the preferred communication method between the various layers of command leading to the front line, as well as specialist users such as the links between artillery observers and their guns — known as the artillery net. Unfortunately, telephone lines proved very susceptible to destruction by enemy artillery and boots and vehicles on the friendly side of the line. Closer to the front line, the enemy could also intercept communication by various means, including simply wrapping his own line around an existing enemy one. The laying of telephone line was a major commitment by both sides and was even carried out under enemy fire during a battle to try to maintain communication. During an attack, telephone contact between the advancing troops and the rear command was never satisfactorily established and other, more time honoured methods, such as runners, pigeons, messenger dogs, signal rockets, Very pistols and flares became the primary method of communication. Primitive radios were used increasingly as the technology improved but no equivalent of the light portable man-pack radio was developed during this war. The power buzzer — which transmitted pulses into the earth — was a very common communication device but encryption became important as the enemy could read the signals easily from his side of No Man's Land (surprise at Fromelles was lost because Australian and British officers discussed the battle in clear language over telephone lines that had been intercepted by the enemy). Various means of communicating with friendly aircraft — known as contact aircraft — were devised, from simple measures such as attaching coloured metal discs to the back of the assaulting infantryman's uniform to the use of coloured smoke signals. The problem with all these methods was timeliness and the amount of detail that could be included. For a commander to influence the outcome of a battle, he needed to know more than basic information such as where his leading troops appeared to be. He needed to know their condition and what they required in terms of reinforcements or supply. He needed to know that they had found a weak point and could exploit it or that they were being held up by a strong point and needed artillery support to overcome it. The communication systems available to the commander in this war never provided that degree of tactical control and flexibility.

# Mining

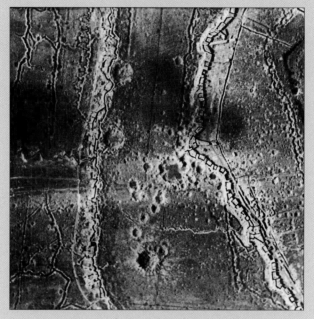

An aerial view taken during the 5th Australian Division's tour of the line showing mine craters between the German and Australian lines, 2,000 yards north of Fromelles. AWM J03376

Mining was one of the less well known methods of waging war on the Western Front. Mining, the digging of tunnels beneath the enemy's front line, filling them with explosives and then detonating them — often to coincide with an attack — was a very old military technique largely rendered obsolete by mobile warfare. Because mining takes so long, it is very much a feature of static warfare, such as siege warfare or the trench warfare of 1915 to 1917. The most famous example of mining, the explosion of nineteen very large mines under the German front lines at the commencement of the Battle of Messines in June 1917, was the culmination of nearly two years of mining activity in the sector. Both sides used mining as a weapon, both offensively and defensively. On the first day of the Somme, the British exploded several large mines under the enemy front line to destroy strong points and disrupt the defenders, with limited success. Mines were also used to try to provide a secure flank to an offensive on a limited front, such as occurred on the left flank of the Australian attack at Fromelles. In the BEF, the tunnelling and mining companies were regarded as strategic assets and were moved around the front to support planned major attacks or defend important sectors of the line.

## Lesson

Given that a significant proportion of the British and Australian casualties resulted from friendly artillery fire, the first lesson is that irrespective of the military imperative, untrained troops will always compromise the potential for success. Had this attack truly set out to capture the objectives set, artillery resources from divisions already skilled and experienced in providing close support should have been allocated.

With known limitations in the available means of communication, commanders needed some method of judging progress other than the observations of returning wounded. The battle reports suggest that there was too much reliance on signal discs and similar practices, although little is recorded of the use of other methods. A multiplicity of methods would have added complexity but also essential redundancy. Other systems available included coloured rockets/Very pistol flares and aerial spotting. Without question, the combination of poor artillery and poor communication compromised the plan's chances of success and contributed directly to heavy casualties in the forming-up phase. These basic battlefield command and communication problems were largely resolved by 1918.

## The Assault Phase

The six o'clock lift of the artillery barrage from the enemy's forward trenches to engage the German communication zones and artillery in the rear area was the general signal for the infantry, now assembled in No Man's Land, to attack.

## 182nd Brigade

On the right of the assault line, the 2/7th Warwicks of the 182nd Brigade were the most fortunate of all the assembling troops. Comparatively unscathed by enemy artillery fire and with minimal small arms fire to disrupt them, they had only fifty metres to charge when the barrage lifted. The enemy line was partially destroyed and thinly held. The forward trench was filled with dead and dazed German defenders and D and C Companies, the two assault companies of the 2/7th, quickly occupied a 200-metre section. The bombers turned left and began to work their way towards the trenches in the 2/6th zone to establish a solid line. Flank protection was employed along the Fauquissart–Trivelet Road while the remaining attackers pushed on towards the main objective, the enemy's support line. Following closely behind were the support troops of B Company and a section of the 182nd Machine Gun Company.It was standard defensive practice for both sides to establish strong defensive belts of barbed wire between the front and rear trench systems. By 1916, both protagonists understood that breaking into an enemy's forward trench was not a major tactical problem; rather the real challenge lay in exploiting this break-in and moving into the rear zone. One of the main benefits of aerial reconnaissance was the detection of these inter-zone defences and the reporting of their position to the artillery so they could be destroyed by the barrage prior to an attack. The surviving assault troops of D and C Companies discovered that the guns had failed to destroy these defences and their movement to the rear was blocked by uncut wire. The enemy had also blocked the communication trenches between the forward and rear lines with prepared balls of tangled barbed wire that they had pulled from the sides of the narrow trenches. To prevent the attackers pulling them away, these obstacles were often covered by enemy small arms fire.

The Warwicks found themselves in a trap. They couldn't move forward and the attackers on their left had not advanced to protect that flank. On their other flank, and from the enemy's rear defence zones to the Warwicks' front and right, German machine-gunners were freed by the lifting of the barrage. Two German guns located in a strong point to the west of the Fauquissart Road and not under direct infantry assault, were able to catch the Warwicks in enfilade taking a terrible toll on the attacking troops caught in front of the uncut wire. The Warwicks frantically attacked the wire and managed to make enough holes for a small number to

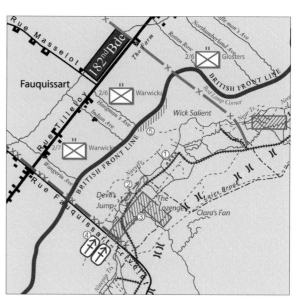

182nd Brigade final phase.
(Mark Wahlert)

scramble into the support trench. The 2/6th had reached its objective. Now it had to hold it.

B Company, trying to work forward into the captured line, was caught in enfilade by these same enemy guns which inflicted heavy casualties. The machine-gun section was reduced from four to just two guns and was quickly overwhelmed. German artillery rejoined the battle and shellfire was so heavy in No Man's Land that reinforcements could not move forward — nor could the survivors of the attack move back. Despite its promising start, by 7.00 pm the 2/7th attack was barely hanging on to its success. It now depended on others.

The second half of the brigade attack, by the 2/6th Warwicks, had started badly. Having lost all its officers to the heavy shelling as they exited their front line, the 2/6th had, nonetheless, managed to assemble an assault force less than eighty metres from the German front line. When the barrage lifted, they were engaged in a deadly race with the defenders to see who could reach the parapets first. German artillery and machine-guns from flanking and rearwards positions assisted in slowing the British advance and it was the Germans who were able to man the machine-guns first. The attack by the 2/6th was now doomed and the presence of the Wick salient effectively sealed its fate. These immensely strong positions provided the Germans with shelter from all but the heaviest shells. But it was a relatively small group of Germans with three machine-guns who had survived the bombardment who gained the parapets while the British were still fifty metres short and who destroyed the attack. A small number of 2/6th attackers, about the equivalent of two platoons, managed to enter the enemy front trenches but they were quickly overcome and either killed, captured or ejected back into the maelstrom of No Man's Land. The battalion objective, the enemy's support line, was never threatened.

With the assaulting companies unable to move forward, B Company, the support company, was caught in the open and suffered heavy casualties. Without B Company however, the two assaulting companies lacked sufficient men to attempt a recapture of the front trench. Many of the survivors began to trickle back to their start lines, while others were pinned down in the open in front of the Wick salient. The attack by the 2/6th was over within half an hour of its start and its failure had severe consequences for the battalions on either side.

## 183rd Brigade

The right-hand battalion, the 2/6th Glosters, faced a formidable obstacle in attaining its objectives. The battalion forming-up process had been disrupted and its two assault companies then faced a largely undamaged German parapet, uncut wire and an alert Wick salient garrison behind its right flank. The few attackers who survived the forming-up phase managed to mount an attack as the barrage lifted and occupy a short length of the enemy's front trench, ironically, close to the Wick salient. They were too few and too disorganised to secure their gains. As the support company had already been committed to the attack to make up numbers in the two assault companies, there was no reserve and, by now, the Germans were sweeping No Man's Land with machine-gun fire from a number of directions. The Battalion Commanding Officer was among the wounded and the Germans maintained their fire on the sally ports, effectively preventing any further reinforcements from moving forward. By 6.30 pm, the 2/6th had reached the limit of its advance.

As noted earlier, the 2/4th Glosters had been severely mauled during the forming-up phase. Even though they faced a reduced company of the *3/16th Bavarian Reserve Infantry Regiment*, losses in the assaulting infantry ranks from artillery fire and flanking machine-guns were more than sufficient to equalise the imbalance. While exact details are difficult to establish, it is clear that the 2/4th did not come close to the German front-line trenches. While there was some movement in No Man's Land in the ten minutes between the lifting of the barrage to start the assault and the decision by the Commanding Officer to abandon any further advance, the battalion was effectively knocked out of the battle before it started.

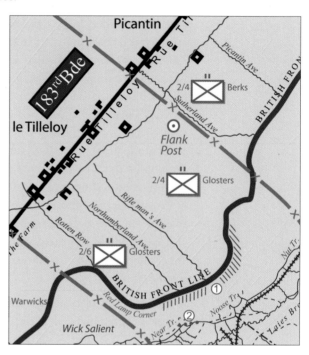

183rd Brigade final phase. (Mark Wahlert)

This left the German defenders in the trench in front of them free to engage the flanks of the two assaulting battalions alongside the 2/4th.

# Machine-gun, Vickers, Mk 1

(Mark Wahlert)

| | |
|---|---|
| **Calibre:** | 0.303in (7.7mm) |
| **Length:** | 1.156m |
| **Weight:** | 18.14kg |
| **Action:** | Recoil |
| **Rate of fire:** | Cyclic – 600rpm |
| **Feed system:** | 250 round, cloth belt |
| **Effective Range:** | 1800m |
| **Manufacturer:** | Vickers, Son & Maxim; Royal Ordnance Factories |

The Vickers was an evolution of the earlier Maxim machine-gun and came into service with the British Army in 1912. The Vickers Mk I was the standard British and Australian medium machine-gun throughout the First and Second World Wars, the Korean War and into the 1960s. It was an extremely reliable weapon — in one instance in World War One, a Vickers fired an average of 10,000 rounds an hour for twelve hours with no stoppages. Heavy and cumbersome to transport, the Vickers was better suited to static warfare as was discovered in France. Initially, Vickers machine-guns were issued to battalions on a standard basis of four per unit. Experience early in the war saw the guns withdrawn from the battalions in early 1916 and combined into machine-gun companies which were a formation rather than a unit asset (known as 'brigade troops'). Later in the war they were reorganised into machine-gun battalions as a divisional resource ('div troops'). In 1915, the machine-gun specialists formed their own corps, the Machine Gun Corps, which was raised in October 1915 and disbanded in 1922.

## 184th Brigade

The forming-up phase was, as previously noted, a disaster for the assaulting troops. Casualties among officers and NCOs left many of the waves leaderless — a compounding disaster for such an inexperienced force.

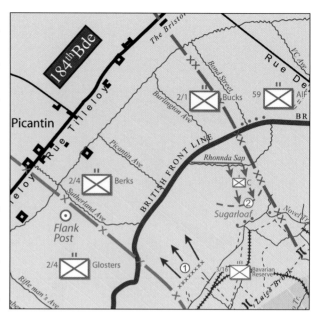

184th Brigade final phase.
(Mark Wahlert)

The 2/4th Berks were to seize the trenches immediately south-west of the Sugarloaf and isolate the position. But the assault companies were so severely reduced during the forming-up stage that, even when reinforced by the reserve company, they lacked the numbers to advance when the barrage lifted. A Company, on the 2/4th left, was annihilated, while B Company on the right managed to gather some small groups and begin the advance. They soon discovered that the wire defending the enemy's front-line trenches was uncut. The survivors, under fire from all sides, failed to breach the wire. Those who could then tried to regain their own lines. (Point 1 in map.)

The 2/1st Bucks, the battalion with the critical job of capturing the Sugarloaf itself, was also savaged while forming up. When the barrage lifted, only 120 men of A and D Companies remained to mount the attack. Initially required to attack across 400 metres of No Man's Land, the Rhondda Sap provided them at least 200 metres of covered approach. However, 120 men required to advance over even 200 metres of open ground and occupy 200 metres of enemy trench were never likely to succeed. The mathematics simply did not work for the 2/1st Bucks. Insufficient numbers without external support, facing a well-entrenched and alert enemy would require more than luck to succeed. They were not lucky. The Germans had the Rhondda Sap well registered with artillery and machine-guns so that, when the barrage lifted and the attackers emerged from the cover of the sap, they met the same fate as the others. Mown down in waves and disorganised by shrapnel, the remnants somehow reached the Sugarloaf and, according to some reports, entered the first line of trenches at 6.10 pm. While the reports may have been accurate, they were also misleading, as there were insufficient attackers to threaten the position. The Sugarloaf continued to function as intended. One tragic outcome of these reports was the 6.10 decision to send forward C Company, the battalion reserve. Of the attackers, nothing more was heard while the unrelenting enemy machine-gun fire quickly destroyed C Company before it reached even the outer wire of the Sugarloaf. (Point 2 on the map.) By 6.30 pm, it was clear to all those left in the front line that the attack on the Sugarloaf had failed: the evidence for this assessment was the continuous heavy enemy fire emanating from both sides of the salient.

## 15th Australian Brigade

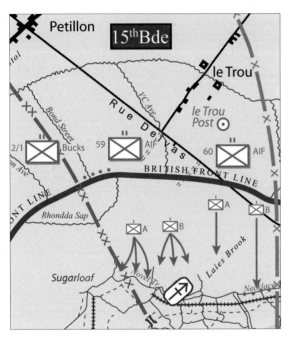

15th Brigade final phase.
(Mark Wahlert)

If the attack by the 184th Brigade was the crucial attack of the operation, it was the 15th Australian Brigade which would be most affected by the outcome of that attack. The 15th was required to advance across the front of the northern and north-eastern fixed fire lanes from the Sugarloaf and attack the trenches to its east. If the 184th failed, there was nothing to prevent the German machine-gunners firing along the lines of the attacking Australian infantry and the 15th Brigade, as the closest, was the obvious target.

The 15th Brigade formed up in No Man's Land with the 59th Battalion on the right and closest to the Sugarloaf and the 60th Battalion alongside on the left. The 15th had moved into No Man's Land with few losses to enemy small arms fire and was formed up ready to launch the assault when the barrage lifted. However, the lifting of the barrage at 6.02 pm was also the signal for the Germans to begin firing. The approach of the first wave of the 59th, about 150 metres from the outer trenches, had been protected by some broken grassy ground. With the lifting of the barrage and their own forward movement, however, they came into sight of both Naval and Necklace Trenches to their front and the machine-gunners in the Sugarloaf itself.

At this stage, the 59th was moving across the face of the Sugarloaf, providing the machine-guns with an ideal target as they fired down a long line of slow-moving men. A Company, on the right of the assault and closest to the Sugarloaf, pushed a few isolated soldiers into the 141

German first-line trenches but, as with the British to their right, lack of numbers and follow-on support meant these few invaders were quickly subdued or killed. The surviving elements of the 59th Battalion were driven back to take cover in shallow depressions in the ground, in some places almost 100 metres short of their first objective.

The story was the same for the 60th Battalion. A few soldiers from the extreme left of the line were reported to have gained the enemy lines, but again, too few and too isolated, they were easy targets for local German counter-attacks. Most of the 60th Battalion survivors of the front waves were driven off and forced to dig shallow scrapes for protection from the devastating machine-gun and artillery fire. For many of these survivors, there was little prospect of a safe withdrawal to their own lines. In addition to the exposed open ground, they had to recross the Laies Brook, the shallow stream that ran parallel to the British lines and along which the Germans had positioned machine-guns which fired on fixed lines.

The 15th Brigade Machine Gun Company, sited between the 184th and 15th Brigades to suppress fire from the Sugarloaf, had been hit hard by the German bombardment during the forming-up phase and, consequently, lost the machine-gun duel. With the failure of their machine-gun cover, the only support available to the Australians as they renewed the attack or withdrew was artillery. Artillery support, however, was not an option. Even had the necessary detailed knowledge of the battlefield situation been available to brigade headquarters to enable such a request to be made, the close proximity of the survivors to the enemy lines and the inexperience of the gunners meant close support shooting by the artillery was out of the question.

The confusion of the battle, combined with some isolated reports of success, provided the 15th Brigade's commander an early and optimistic assessment of progress. At 6.30 pm he reported to the Divisional Commander that his Brigade's attack had been successful. Ten minutes later, he received the first intimation that his assessment was premature when a surviving officer from the 59th Battalion reported its true position. Other information at first led Elliott to believe that only the 59th had faltered but, by 7.20 pm, he realised that the entire brigade attack had failed with heavy losses. At the time of his 6.30 report, almost all the officers and NCOs of both his battalions had become casualties. From the 59th Battalion alone, thirty-five of the thirty-nine officers involved were dead or wounded.

# 15cm *lang schwere feldhaubitze* 1913 (lg SFH13)

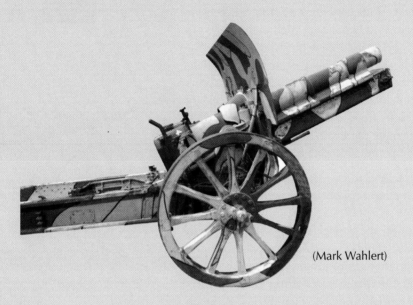

(Mark Wahlert)

| | |
|---|---|
| **Calibre:** | 149.7mm (5.89in) |
| **Weight:** | 2.2 tonnes |
| **Length:** | 2.54m |
| **Crew**: | six |
| **Rate of Fire:** | 3rpm |
| **Effective Range**: | 8600m |
| **Manufacturer:** | Krupp, Rheinmetall, Spandau |

The 15cm *lang schwere feldhaubitze* (long heavy field howitzer), or 15cm SFH 13, was a development of earlier Krupp-designed heavy howitzers. On the outbreak of World War One this gun was immediately deployed and gave the Germans a major firepower advantage on the Western Front in the early part of the war, as the French and British lacked an equivalent weapon. It was not until late 1915 that the British deployed their own 6-inch howitzer. The German SFH13 was a very steady and accurate gun, and was the backbone of the German artillery regiments by the opening of the Somme Offensive in 1916. About 3,500 were produced from 1913 to 1918. The British referred to these guns and their shells as '5 point 9s', or '5 9s', as the bore was 5.9 inches (150mm). The 5.9 was also referred to as a 'Jack Johnson' (a particularly dark-skinned American boxer known as 'the big smoke') or a 'coal box', owing to the large volume of black smoke produced by its high explosive shells.

## 14th Australian Brigade

On the left of the 15th and in the middle of the three attacking Australian brigades, the 14th Brigade should have benefitted from secure flank protection. With the failure of the 15th Brigade attack, the 53rd Battalion, which was on the 14th Brigade's right flank, was exposed to fire from the Sugarloaf and the enemy trenches on its north-eastern approaches behind the 53rd Battalion's right flank. Some fire came also from Necklace Trench to its front, although the British barrage had been more successful in this sector during the forming-up and advance stages.

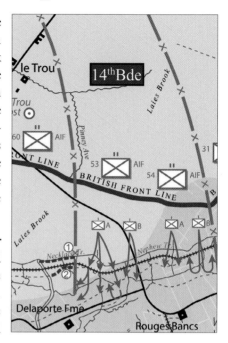

14th Brigade final phase.
(Mark Wahlert)

Having weathered the artillery and *minenwerfer* fire during the initial phase, the battalion managed to manoeuvre sufficient A Company survivors close behind the barrage so that, when it lifted, they could clamber quickly across the parapets to engage the enemy infantry in hand-to-hand fighting. Driving off or killing the machine-gunners to their front provided the assault waves some relief and, once they had entered the German trenches, they were protected from the enfilade fire from the Sugarloaf and the western end of Necklace Trench. Unfortunately for the overall success of the attack, these well-placed machine-guns were then able to play a major role in destroying the follow-up waves still in No Man's Land and preventing the movement of reinforcements or resupply to sustain the advance.

The first waves caught some of the defenders emerging from their shelters and killed most of them, driving the others from the front-line breastworks. On A Company's left, B Company and the two assault companies from the 54th Battalion had a slightly easier approach and quickly overran the undamaged enemy breastworks, advancing to the second line, a more substantial trench system known as the *Wohngraben*. The attack by the 14th Brigade appeared to be going well but, as Pedersen notes, the seeds of the problem had already been sown by the initial toll of casualties. While the brigade's overall casualties had been comparatively light, almost all its leaders had been killed or wounded. The Battalion Commander of the 53rd, Lieutenant Colonel I. B. Norris, and his staff managed to cross No Man's Land safely to the security of the first trench but, as they moved further forward to the enemy support line, an unsuppressed machine-gun engaged and killed or wounded the entire party. Given other officer losses, command of the 53rd was assumed by a young captain who, while keen and enthusiastic, had little experience or training for such a role. The men of the 14th Brigade now on the German side of No Man's Land were essentially leaderless.

The 14th Brigade's objective was the support line in the German defences and the attacking waves rolled on, expecting at any moment to find another substantial system that resembled the one they had just captured. Instead they encountered a patchwork of open, grassed fields, hedges, trees and drainage ditches. While some of the ditches were agricultural, many others were the remnants of defensive works from the previous year, abandoned when the Laies flooded them and then left to become overgrown and rank. The confusion between what the photo interpreters saw and what the assault troops found is understandable, although Bean is critical of the slowness of the British General Staff to develop specialist photo interpreters to assist the intelligence process.

The men of the 14th Brigade advanced over 300 metres in some instances, and a few reportedly even advanced 600 metres, although their orders had told them that the final objective was closer than 250 metres. Consequently, the attackers became disorganised, separated and, in some cases, disoriented and lost. Some advanced through their own protective barrage as it fell on the German approach lines, while others crossed Rue Delvas, well beyond the objective. Had more officers survived, the advance may have halted earlier when it became apparent that the objective did not exist. The few who did survive set about withdrawing their men to the comparative safety of the captured enemy line and converting it to a defensive position.

The 53rd was still receiving enemy fire on its flank and had to bend its right flank back to provide some protection. Beyond the right flank, a small party of bombers from the 53rd struggled to fend off the Germans advancing from the trenches to their right — the trenches that the 60th Battalion was to have secured. By 7.00 pm, these men were unable to hold on and, taking with them twenty German prisoners and a few men of the 60th Battalion who had joined them, pulled back to their own lines. This withdrawal prompted other retirements by troops engaged in digging communication trenches in No Man's Land and a major disaster was averted only by the arrival of reinforcements from the 55th Battalion. The 14th Brigade's most pressing problem, however, was once again a matter of communication: while the Brigade Commander and eventually the Divisional Commander were aware of the now unprotected flank of the 53rd Battalion, the commander in the front line and most of his men were not.

On its left flank, the 54th Battalion had been forced out of the German second-line trenches by Australian artillery fire and was consolidating in the front-line breastworks. Ironically, in view of the popular image of the muddy Western Front battlefields, the consolidation effort was hampered by thick dust thrown up by the artillery. Despite the confusion, the heavy losses and the severe shortage of leaders, by 6.30 pm the 14th Brigade had established the semblance of a defensive position within its section of captured German lines. Now the challenge was to defend its gains.

## 8th Australian Brigade

The heavy casualties inflicted on the 8th Brigade by both the enemy and its own artillery during the initial phases profoundly affected its ability to consolidate its gains and support its men in their exposed forward positions. As both the attacking battalions had suffered the greatest proportion of their total losses in the pre-assault phases, numbers were clearly going to be a problem, especially in the later phases when the German tactic of using artillery to isolate attacking groups from their support meant they had to defend their gains with little hope of reinforcement.

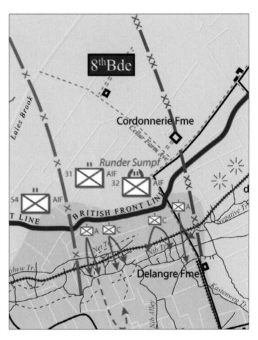

8th Brigade break-in phase.
(Mark Wahlert)

The narrow width of No Man's Land enabled the 8th Brigade to reach the enemy front trenches in sufficient strength to drive off the defenders. Small groups of individuals paused to engage the Australians with grenades before retreating or seeking shelter in dugouts. The fighting became a confused skirmish through the front trench system and around traverses, the Australians engaging scattered parties of the enemy as they emerged from their shelters. Much effort was devoted to bombing attacks on the enemy's deep shelters. The artillery continued to fire on the trenches and men from both sides were killed by the same shrapnel explosions. Many of the defenders retreated from the support trench system into the open country behind, making their way back to the enemy's second-line defences higher up the ridgeline. While the enemy machine-gun fire from the left flank continued to inflict casualties, the capture of the front-line trench system provided the supporting waves some respite and the crossing of No Man's Land was marginally easier for the follow-up waves.

The successful capture of the front trench system enabled the assault waves to continue the advance and, like the 14th Brigade to its right, the 8th discovered that the next objective did not exist. The anticipated network of trenches and breastworks could not be found. The high rate of casualties forced the 31st Battalion Commander, Lieutenant Colonel F.W. Toll, to leave the defence of the trenches to his few Lewis gun teams while he took his surviving troops out into the grass to find the next objective. For a brief period, the 31st advanced at an almost leisurely pace until they came across a deep ditch, filled with stagnant water. While clearly not an enemy trench, it was obviously substantial enough to resemble a trench on aerial photographs or through the binoculars of observers in reconnaissance balloons.

Uncertain as to whether this was the enemy second line that formed his objective, Toll decided to press on with the advance. After advancing another 200 metres, he found nothing of tactical value except an elementary shallow sap where he decided to establish his defensive line. He sent back a message that stated, '6.30 pm. Four waves well over 200 yards beyond enemy's parapets. No enemy works found yet so am digging in.' Leaving his troops to establish the line and try to contact the attackers on either flank, Toll pushed on with his intelligence officer and a messenger to ensure the objective wasn't just a bit further forward. Advancing another 200 metres, he found nothing that resembled his objective, although he did discover the enemy strong point known as the *Grashof*. Returning to his defensive line, he found that his battalion had still not contacted troops on either flank, although small parties of both could be seen.

Continued artillery fire, both enemy and friendly, began to reveal the weakness of Toll's exposed position. When enemy troops were spotted manoeuvring behind his flank, he quickly realised that his position was untenable and, at 7.00 pm, withdrew his troops to the old German front line. He left a small advance party in the open area in a trench which extended parallel to the main German line into the area of the 32nd Battalion. It was through this minor position that the 31st and 32nd finally established contact and formed a defensive position. Unknown to Toll, this forward line was also on the same basic alignment as the forward elements of the 54th Battalion of 14 Brigade on his right. They were separated by a gap of over 300 metres.

On Toll's left, and on the extreme left of the entire attack, the 32nd was experiencing the same problems finding its next objective. The only defence works of substance appeared to be a long, well-built communication trench on the left flank, later identified as the *Kastenweg*. This trench, which connected the front trench system to the strong defences around Delangré Farm, was immediately converted to flank protection. The advancing infantry then moved another 300 metres to the rear through the same wasteland of long grass and watery ditches until they realised that they had gone beyond their intended objectives. On the left flank, some of the 32nd attempted to capture Delangré Farm itself but it was too well defended and the attack failed. Unable to locate any defensible feature that resembled their objective, the 32nd survivors under their remaining officer, Major J.J. Hughes, concluded that the ditches to the rear of the captured front trench must have been the objective and set about establishing a defence line.

## Summary

While the outcome of the attack was decided within an hour of the commencement of the assault, it took the commanders of both divisions some time to appreciate the real situation. Major General Mackenzie (see biographical notes) of the 61st, however, was able to review his division's position a little earlier. By 6.30 pm, less than half an hour after the attack had commenced, he became aware that his troops had not achieved the anticipated result. His right-hand brigade had gained half of its objectives but had failed to capture the Wick salient and was under heavy fire. His central brigade had essentially failed, with only a small group of attackers having gained the enemy lines north-east of the Wick salient. The crucial left attack had also faltered. While he had received reports that some assault troops had entered the Sugarloaf, the enemy positions there continued to operate and were clearly untroubled by any attackers.

The reports received by the Australian commander were much more positive. By 7.30 pm, he had been informed that the 14th Brigade was 150 metres past the old German front line and digging in, while the 8th Brigade occupied a similar position. The 8th Brigade's primary concern was the security of its flanks. Of greater concern to McCay, Commander of the 5th Australian Division (see biographical notes), was the situation on his right flank. It was assumed, but not confirmed, that some of the 60th Battalion had entered the enemy line. However, it was clear to all that the 59th had failed to make any impression on the Sugarloaf. By eight o'clock, these reports had been received by Corps Headquarters and Haking began planning ways of supporting what local successes had been achieved. In particular, he looked to reinforce the success — as he understood it — of the 2/1st Bucks at the Sugarloaf.

# Officers' Weapons

Officers were supposed to lead, plan, encourage and organise, rather than engage directly in the fighting. For this reason, they usually went into battle more lightly armed than the soldiers they led. The standard officer weapon, the revolver, was intended primarily for self-defence. Later in the war, officers were more inclined to dress like their soldiers and carry standard infantry weapons. They did this primarily because carrying a revolver instantly identified them to enemy snipers and made them a priority target. British officers were well served by a reliable revolver.

## Service Revolver, Webley, Mk IV

(Mark Wahlert)

| | |
|---|---|
| **Calibre:** | 0.455in (11.56mm) |
| **Length:** | 286 mm |
| **Weight:** | 1.1 kg, unloaded |
| **Action:** | Double-action revolver |
| **Capacity:** | 6 rounds |
| **Rate of Fire:** | 20 – 30rpm |
| **Effective Range:** | 50m |
| **Manufacturer:** | Webley & Scott, Royal Small Arms Factory, Enfield, UK |

First produced in the 1870s by Webley & Son of Great Britain, the Webley revolver was adopted for British military service in 1887 as a Webley Revolver, 0.455in, Mk I. It was a break-top, six-shot, double-action revolver, which launched a heavy (18gm) lead bullet at relatively slow muzzle velocity (180m per second). The Webley revolver evolved through several marks, with the Mk VI being the standard sidearm of the British Empire forces in World War One. In fact, the Mks IV, V and VI were all in use during World War One, but the long-barrelled Mk VI, as the latest version, was probably the most commonly seen. It remained in use for the duration of the war, and was issued to officers, airmen, naval crews, boarding parties, trench-raiders, machine-gun teams and tank crews. The Mk VI proved to be a very reliable and hardy weapon, well suited to the mud and adverse conditions of trench warfare, and several accessories were developed for this model, including a bayonet, a speed-loader device, and a stock allowing the revolver to be converted to a carbine.

# Luger P.08 Parabellum Pistol

(Mark Wahlert)

| | |
|---|---|
| **Calibre:** | 7.65mm |
| **Length:** | 222mm |
| **Weight:** | 0.876kg, unloaded |
| **Action:** | Toggle-locked, short recoil |
| **Capacity:** | 8 round detachable straight box magazine |
| **Rate of Fire:** | Semi-automatic |
| **Effective Range:** | 50m (short barrel model) |
| **Manufacturer:** | Deutsche Waffen und Munitionsfabriken (DWM) & numerous others in Germany and under licence abroad |

The P.08, better known simply as the Luger pistol after its designer, Georg Luger, is among the best known handguns ever produced. Initially made in 1900 for the Swiss Army, it was adopted by the German Army in 1908 as its standard issue sidearm. The Luger continued in this role until 1938 when it was replaced by the Walther P.38. While numerous variants had been produced by the time of World War One, the most common military versions were the Army's 4-in barrel, the Navy's 6-in barrel and the artillery 8-in barrel models. The name 'Parabellum' is derived from an ancient Latin axiom, *Si vis pacem, para bellum* — 'if you want peace, prepare for war'. The Luger was a recoil-operated, locked breech, semi-automatic, striker-fired handgun, featuring a unique locking system and short, moving barrel and was well regarded for its accuracy. However, it jammed easily and was expensive to manufacture. Throughout both the First and Second World Wars the Luger was among the most valued souvenirs of the Allied soldier.

# CHAPTER SIX

# THE ATTACK FAILS:
## THE GERMANS COUNTER-ATTACK

By the time General Haking had begun planning to exploit his limited successes, there were few gains on the right half of the attack to exploit, while the position on his left was misleading. The enemy, on the other hand, who had a much clearer picture of the battlefield, was about to reverse the few successes Haking's troops had achieved.

The Germans had acquired a reputation as able exponents of the art of the counter-attack. The counter-attack is one of the most difficult military operations to conduct as it involves retaking territory just captured by the enemy. During World War One, the counter-attack was often conducted as the enemy's attack continued. Counter-attacks were designed to strike the advancing enemy when he was tired, disorganised, caught in the open or in damaged and broken defences, and well below combat strength due to losses in the attack. A well-conducted counter-attack had the potential not only to recapture lost territory, but to inflict disproportionately large losses on the attacker. But it was a difficult action to execute, requiring precise coordination between the infantry and the artillery, clear communication between all levels of command and adjoining formations and, above all, sound initiative on the part of the counter-attacking troops, particularly their junior leaders.

At Fromelles, the Germans enjoyed some major advantages over the attacking forces. As they had been defending an established position for some time, their telephone lines were deeply buried and less vulnerable to destruction. Their artillery had every part of their own front line registered and ranged. The German troops, who had occupied that section of the front for months, were intimately acquainted with the pattern of trenches and shelters. Finally, having watched the build-up and the assault, they knew the enemy they were facing. Once the counter-attacks began, all the advantages lay with the Bavarians.

It was 6.31 pm when the Commanding Officer of the 2/7th Warwicks, Lieutenant Colonel H. Nutt, received a message confirming that his advanced troops were isolated in the enemy's forward trenches. At 6.37 he ordered the construction of a communication trench from his forward line out to his beleaguered men only to find that accurate and heavy German artillery fire thwarted every attempt. A few minutes later he received the grim news by runner that fewer than twenty of his men remained on the objective. Observing the enemy line, he could also see enemy grenade throwers ('bombers') forcing his men back along the trench from the direction of the Wick salient. Both Nutt and the 182nd Brigade Commander, Brigadier General A. Gordon, began bringing up reinforcements to force a connection to the isolated outpost.

Since the German counter-attack had commenced almost as soon as the British had penetrated their front line, however, this was all too little too late. Using combinations of bombers and machine-gunners, German junior officers such as Lieutenant Schattenman organised defences that pinned the attackers in set localities while other Germans manoeuvred onto the flanks and to the rear of the attackers. The surviving defenders of the initial British attack were rallied and formed into composite bombing teams while others moved in from the flanks. The Fauquissart–Trivelet Road provided no protection and attempts by the Warwicks to block its approaches with small parties of riflemen failed. The Warwicks were quickly assailed by counter-attacks from both flanks and in front and, by 7.45 pm, the entire captured position was back in German hands. To compound the attackers' failure, the Germans turned two of the captured Vickers machine-guns on their previous owners.

In the centre, no contact had been established with the small party of the 2/4th Glosters who had reportedly entered the enemy lines just north of the Wick salient. There are no accounts yet translated that describe how the Bavarian defenders dealt with this incursion. However, it is possible to extrapolate from the experience of the 2/7th Warwicks on the other side of the Wick salient. The German local commanders would have reacted immediately, organising groups of bombers to counter-attack by 'rolling up' the disorganised Glosters from the right flank. Whatever the method, by the time the brigade and divisional commanders began to plan to exploit their success at 6.30, it was likely that none of the Glosters in the enemy trenches was still fighting.

The other success reported to the higher command, the penetration of the Sugarloaf by the 2/1st Bucks, was even less open to exploitation. By the time Mackenzie conducted his 6.30 pm review, he had received reports that there were British troops on the objective — despite the fact that the empirical evidence indicated that there was no success to reinforce. Under pressure from the Australians to neutralise the Sugarloaf and exhorted by Corps Headquarters to try again on the other objectives, Mackenzie had little option but to plan a new attack.

The artillery's failure even to cut the wire satisfactorily was by now abundantly clear. Reports from the wounded were painting a grim picture of uncut wire, undamaged enemy breastworks and untroubled machine-gun positions. German artillery and *minenwerfer* continued to deny No Man's Land to work and resupply parties. The higher command now realised that a renewed artillery bombardment of the unsuppressed enemy strong points was the highest priority if the attack was to maintain its apparent momentum. Mackenzie ordered a new bombardment of the Wick salient and those sections of the line where his assault troops had been repelled. However, he could not order a bombardment of those parts of the trench-line he believed his troops still occupied. The war diary records do not indicate whether the Sugarloaf was initially included in the bombardment plan although, by 7.30 pm, when the higher command realised that there were no friendly troops on the Sugarloaf, it had been added to the target list. The bombardment was to begin at 7.10 pm and last an hour. Mackenzie also ordered another attack to follow the end of the bombardment and Haking approved the use of the reserve for this assault. Under the protection of the bombardment, those troops who had been pinned down in No Man's Land scrambled back to the safety of their trenches.

Given the limited number of divisions allocated to the attack, and the use of all three brigades in the first assault, there were few fresh troops to provide the essential mass for a renewed attack. The 182nd Brigade was restricted to using the reserve company of the 2/7th Warwicks to attempt to force through and link up with the remnants believed to be holding the enemy front line. The 183rd Brigade assembled its reserve companies for a renewed attempt when the barrage lifted. The belated decision to include the Sugarloaf in the pre-attack artillery preparations now saw the renewed attack postponed until 9.00 pm to coincide with the revised timing of the new divisional attack.

The confusion over the reality of the situation on the division's left flank provides the final chapter of the 61st Division's story in this battle. The problems with communication between the differing levels of command had resulted in the divisional and brigade commanders having a different appreciation of the situation from that of the 2/1st Bucks' Commanding Officer in the front line. This misunderstanding was compounded when orders were issued for a new attack. Lieutenant Colonel Williams of the Bucks was unable to convince his brigadier that the penetration of the Sugarloaf was not as effective as originally reported or that he had insufficient troops to mount a renewed assault. Eventually about eighty men were assembled from the ranks of the survivors and from the reserve battalion to try once again to capture the Sugarloaf. As further evidence of the confusion, the 61st Division advised the Australian command of the renewed attack and asked them to assist. This request was handed to the 15th Australian Brigade Commander at 8.10 pm.

# *Minenwerfer* (mine launcher)

The *minenwerfer*, or mine launcher, was a German short-range mortar used extensively during World War One by the German Army. The *minenwerfer* was intended for use by engineers to clear obstacles including bunkers and barbed wire that longer range artillery could not accurately target. Built in three sizes prior to the war, in 1914 the German Army was able to field a large mortar (*schwerer minenwerfer*) of 250mm calibre, a medium version (the 170mm *mittlerer minenwerfer*) and a light mortar (the 75.8mm *leichter minenwerfer*). From the size and shape of their bombs, which could often be seen in flight, the medium and heavy devices were generally referred to as 'rum jars' or as 'minnies' by the British. These weapons proved far more efficient than artillery in the static warfare that gripped the Western Front. Unlike field artillery, the light *minenwerfer* could be moved around the battlefield by four men, was cheaper to produce and was more accurate. As an indication of the weapon's success, by 1918 there were 1,234 heavy, 2,361 medium and 12,329 light *minenwerfers* deployed. A 380mm very heavy mine launcher (*sehr schwerer minenwerfer*) was also developed.

77mm German light trench mortar.
(Photos courtesy of the Australian War Memorial)

Before the new attack began, the Corps Commander finally received a realistic picture of the true state of the 61st Division. Deciding it could not recommence the attack, he countermanded the scheduled 9.00 pm assault and ordered the three British brigades to withdraw their troops to their original lines. At this point, Haking was still considering a renewal of the attack the following morning and asked the 5th Division for a report on what it had achieved. He directed that all ground captured be consolidated and held. A little later, a contact aeroplane reported that flares had been seen in and around the Sugarloaf, and in areas well into the German lines behind the other Australian brigade positions. This information, which appeared to contradict the reports of the ground observers, prompted Haking to switch the emphasis of the attack. The Australians were to hold their gains while the British would renew their endeavours to seize the Sugarloaf the next day.

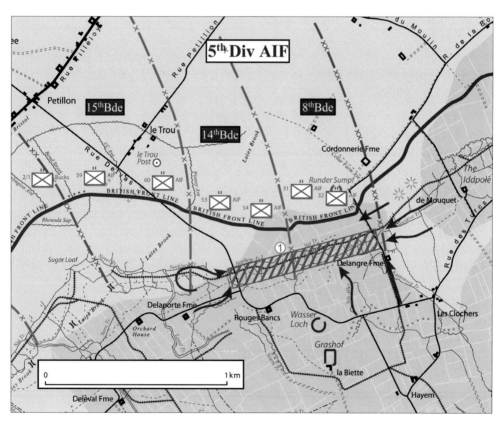

General area occupied by the Australians. German counter-attacks shown as red arrows.
(Mark Wahlert)

155

Despite the losses and the confusion, the Australian division had achieved many of its objectives. The only major failure was the 15th Brigade's attack on the Sugarloaf itself. At 7.20 when Elliott had provided his Divisional Commander an assessment of the attack, he was still under the impression that the British battalion on his right had managed to enter the Sugarloaf. However, he now had first-hand evidence that the Germans continued to operate unhindered within their strong point.

The tactical requirement to support the successful Bucks and neutralise the strong point was obvious and both McCay and Elliott began planning further action to secure the Sugarloaf. McCay released his remaining limited reinforcements to his brigades at 7.40 pm, hoping that the infusion of men would provide the necessary mass to move the line forward. Elliott received his reinforcements around the same time as the requests for a renewed coordinated attack against the Sugarloaf arrived from the 184th Brigade. He immediately proposed sending half his reinforcements forward to join the remnants of the 59th Battalion in No Man's Land so they would be in position to launch a new assault when the barrage lifted at 9.00 pm. He brought the other half up from the reserve trenches to provide support once the assault went in.

Unknown to Elliott, Haking had decided to cancel the new assault. He issued orders to McCay not to use any more troops to reinforce the failure in the 15th Brigade zone and to withdraw any men who remained isolated in No Man's Land. The focus for the 5th Division was to be the consolidation of the two successful attacks by the 14th and 8th Brigades.

Unlike the 61st Division, Elliott was not informed of the cancellation of the 9.00 pm attack. The 5th Division itself only became aware of the order at 8.35 pm and did not move quickly enough to pass on the information. At 9.00 pm, two companies of the 58th Battalion, the new reinforcements, together with some survivors of the earlier attack by the 59th, rose up from the grass and began to advance the remaining 200 metres to the Sugarloaf. In Bean's words 'there was opened from the salient a fire of machine guns so severe that the line was shattered and the men dazed.' The attack was a complete disaster. Without the distraction of assaults from several directions and with little artillery fire on them, the German defenders were free to concentrate their full effort on the small number of attacking troops. Post-war surveys of the battlefield found evidence that a few individuals had made it to the parapet of the Sugarloaf but most remains were found in rows more than 100 metres short of the objective.

While the right flank of the Australian line was being destroyed, the rest of the division was working to consolidate and expand their local successes. At 10.30 pm, McCay asked each of his brigadiers whether, if allocated some reserves, they could capture all their original objectives. Elliott, who continued to believe that his other battalion, the 60th, was occupying part of the German trench to its front, was less than confident in his response: 'GOC cannot guarantee success of attack with 57th Battalion as enemy machine gun fire is very hot, but is willing to try.' It was not until 12.30 am that Elliott learned that the men of the 60th were not in the enemy's trenches but were in effect destroyed, as were the two companies of the 57th who had launched the later attack. He advised McCay of this, adding, 'the attack of this Brigade has completely failed'. McCay moved decisively to recover, immediately instructing Elliott to abandon the attack, retrieve as many of his men as possible and organise the defensive line on his old position. He directed the artillery to fire on the enemy trenches he had previously believed occupied so as to provide flank protection to the 14th Brigade in its captured positions. He also ordered the 15th Brigade to try to push a trench across No Man's Land to connect with the right flank of the 14th Brigade position (this failed as not even the 14th Brigade was sure of the position of its forward troops). For the 15th Brigade, the battle effectively ended at this point. Stragglers and wounded continued to trickle back, but no further offensive action was attempted.

The hours since the success of the 14th Brigade advance had been particularly eventful. Much effort had been devoted to turning captured trenches around to form rudimentary defensive positions. The plan had called for the support troops to construct communication trenches and saps across No Man's Land to the captured positions to aid the build-up of reinforcements and the movement of heavy weapons and engineering supplies to further improve the positions. The failure to suppress the German artillery and, most importantly, the machine-guns in the Sugarloaf, largely prevented this construction, although great effort was expended in digging trenches out into No Man's Land. Construction was also affected by the initial heavy losses which seriously reduced the number of troops available to dig the trenches and carry supplies. The losses among the assault troops also meant that the men delivering ammunition were drafted into the defensive line rather than returning to the rear to continue their resupply. The onset of dusk reduced some of the difficulties of crossing No Man's Land, but at no stage did the resupply and reinforcement system work as intended.

At 9.30 pm, the defenders received some welcome reinforcements from the remaining two companies of the 55th Battalion. One was sent to the left flank to reinforce the 54th Battalion and the other to reinforce the 53rd. These reinforcements allowed the brigade to develop an almost continuous front. The threat was not in front of them, however, but came from their flanks. A sizeable gap existed between the 14th Brigade and the 8th Brigade on their left. On their right flank was an enemy-held trench system. On this flank, three communication trenches running from the German strong point at Rouges Bancs to separate parts of the 14th Brigade's new defensive positions provided the German counter-attack with concealed, protected approaches. The Australian defenders were well aware of these and made every effort to close them off.

By far the most serious threat came from the trenches on the Australians' right flank, exposed initially by the 60th Battalion's inability to capture them and the subsequent withdrawal of the bombers of their own battalion. These trenches had lain empty since then and it was the Germans, probing forward from all points, who were the first to discover and exploit them. As the Germans advanced along the old front-line trenches, they unwittingly moved between the forward defenders of the 53rd and their supporting elements in the former German front-line trenches. Eventually, the Bavarians encountered men working on improving a communication trench and a vicious bomb fight warned the 53rd defenders of the new danger. A spirited defence could not prevent the Germans eventually recapturing the trench and the forward right flank of the brigade was partially cut off. The reinforcing troops from the 55th Battalion, working on developing the position, were forced to abandon their construction work and become fully involved in repelling the advancing Germans.

Part of the problem lay in the fact that, even as late as 10.30 pm, the 14th Brigade officers in the front line remained unaware of the failure of the 15th Brigade to seize its objectives. Several patrols were despatched to try to locate the missing 60th Battalion. By 11.00 pm it had become obvious that the flank approaches had to be stopped and much effort was expended on building 'blocks' in the right-hand trenches. This, together with the temporary exhaustion of the enemy's local reserves, earned the defenders of the right flank some temporary respite. However, the forward positions on this flank remained dangerously exposed.

The rest of the 14th Brigade spent those hours consolidating their defensive positions. Supplies were very low and, with the absorption of the carrying parties into the defending sections, finding men to bring up more ammunition presented a major difficulty. Sandbags were in critically short supply, particularly given their importance for reinforcing the former rear walls of the German trenches. Ammunition, especially grenades, was also running dangerously low. A further problem was the gradual flooding of the trench system as the Laies Brook, blocked in several places, backed up into the trenches. Some of the Australians were convinced that the Germans had deliberately dammed the brook. The rising water added the risk of drowning — especially for wounded men — to the many other hazards the defenders faced.

Following the repulse of their initial counter-attack, the Bavarians began to mount a coordinated divisional response. The divisional reserve, the *Bavarian 14th Reserve Brigade*, was brought forward to the eastern side of the Australian incursion to attack the left-hand edge of the Australian position, that of the 8th Brigade. The *Bavarian 16th Regiment* was to support this attack by exerting pressure on the right-hand end of the line held by the 14th Brigade. The attack began at 11.40 pm with the 14th Brigade registering the first contact. At around 1.00 am, an Australian officer scouting for a better approach to the exposed right-hand positions of the brigade encountered some withdrawing Australian bombers, hotly pursued by the advancing Germans. The 200 defenders in the forward positions were also quickly alerted to the enemy's approach. As the night sky lightened, the defenders saw men moving over the open ground behind them and opened fire. They paused briefly, concerned that they might have been firing on the missing 60th Battalion men, but the fight resumed when bombs and small arms fire proved beyond doubt that these were Germans.

The fighting became more complex and confused as the Germans penetrated more deeply into the gap between the forward elements and the old German front line. The confusion was increased by dust, smoke and the bright light of flares. The Australians, already low on ammunition, began to run short of grenades and the battle began to consume the brigade. More and more defenders were despatched to hold the attack and were never seen again. Officers and NCOs were being shot down at close range from just behind the defensive positions. Communication between the forward positions was only possible through the single improvised trench, while communication with the old German front line and back to their own lines was reduced to a tenuous link of ditches and shell holes. Early in the morning of 20 July, the remnants of the 53rd attempted to stage a breakthrough to the old German front-line trench but failed. Many of the remaining defenders then moved left, joining the 54th, while others, believing that this was a general instruction to retire, began making their own way back to their original lines.

The arrival of the 53rd survivors announced to the 54th that their right flank protection had collapsed. Lieutenant Colonel Cass, Commanding Officer of the 54th Battalion, had been trying to obtain more supplies — particularly of the vital grenades — from the rear when the news of the collapse reached him at around 3.00 am. Some forty-five minutes later, he was advised that the Germans were advancing behind the brigade's position so quickly they were close to severing his last communication link with his own lines. While organising desperate local counter-attacks of his own, Cass also informed his brigade commander at 4.30 am that, with the collapse of the 53rd Battalion, he was close to being surrounded and had to withdraw or he would be cut off. His position worsened as the Germans advanced from the east, entering the gap between the 14th and 8th Brigades. While the left flank, manned by men of the 55th Battalion held, they could not prevent the enemy advancing to the old German front line. The last links between the two brigades had been severed. Fortunately for the 14th, the German attackers turned east and assaulted the right flank of the 8th Brigade.

The plight of the remnants of the 14th Brigade was becoming obvious to all. McCay realised that, with the coming of the dawn, the brigade would be exposed to machine-gun fire from all the enemy trenches from the Sugarloaf east. He ordered a heavy artillery bombardment of these positions to provide some protection until the renewed assault took place. The commanders gathered at 5.00 am to review the position and the bleak news from all sectors, including the 14th Brigade, convinced them to abandon any plans for renewing the attack. A warning was despatched to Cass at 5.15 am to expect an order to retire, although he was told not to do so until advised. He received the warning at 6.30 am, by which time the position had become clear not only to him, but to all the remaining defenders. By this time, the 8th Brigade had also been driven back and the 14th was being assailed from both flanks and by renewed attacks from its front. The retirement of the 8th had a serious effect on the morale of the defenders from the 14th. At 6.30, Cass began to organise a rearguard to cover the retirement of the brigade, including a plan to save the precious machine-guns, but he was still waiting for the formal order to retire from brigade headquarters. Finally, at 7.50 am, the order was received and the withdrawal began. It had taken eight runners to get the message across the inferno that was No Man's Land. Many defenders either did not believe the order or never received it, as large numbers remained at their posts and had to be either driven out or killed by the advancing Germans. Many others hung on until almost surrounded then fought their way out, often in hand-to-hand fighting. The efforts expended in digging saps across No Man's Land during the night paid dividends, as these provided some cover for the retiring men, although the casualties incurred were again very heavy. The return of the 14th Brigade to its lines signalled the end of the fighting, although many more soldiers were still destined to die.

German map showing direction of German counter-attacks. Map supplied
as part of a report by Peter Barton on his research on behalf of the
Australian Army in the *Hauptstaatsarchiv Kriegsarchiv*
in Munich, Germany.

German map showing direction of moves and counter-attacks around the 8th Brigade's position. Map supplied as part of a report by Peter Barton on his research on behalf of the Australian Army in the *Hauptstaatsarchiv Kriegsarchiv* in Munich, Germany.

Although the 14th Brigade was the last to leave the enemy lines, it was the 8th which faced the main German counter-attack in the early hours of 20 July. Its exposed position on the left flank of the attack meant that the 8th Brigade was always going to bear the brunt of any enemy counter-attack. The failure of the various schemes to protect it during the advance and the attack phases merely reinforced its exposure. McCay had recognised its vulnerability, instructing the brigade to exercise special care in building flank protection and blocks at the ends of all captured enemy trenches. Engineers were assigned to the brigade to assist construction of strong points and repair captured trenches. They were also tasked to help speed construction of communication trenches across No Man's Land, as the presence of the enemy on the flanks was always going to make crossing between both trench-lines hazardous. Beyond the enemy front line, the captured *Kastenweg* provided both a strong defensive position and a source of sandbags and construction material to reinforce other parts of the new defences. Parties of bombers and a machine-gun were stationed along this exposed flank but, with the heavy casualties already suffered, the battalion was unable to develop a robust defensive line.

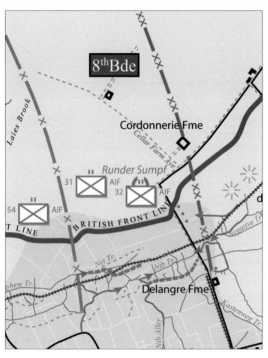

Final position of the 8th Brigade before its retreat to its own lines.
(Mark Wahlert)

As early as 8.30 pm it was becoming apparent to all, except some of those men isolated forward of the captured enemy line, that the expected German counter-attack against the exposed left flank was developing. With daylight fading, enemy artillery fire on the 8th Brigade position increased and bombing from the front and side escalated. Fresh enemy troops were observed gathering around Delangré Farm in increasing numbers. Shortly after dusk, the first serious counter-attack was launched on the left of the 32nd Battalion, the attackers emerging from the unoccupied part of the *Kastenweg* and from the adjacent trenches in the former front line. Calls for artillery assistance again saw the Australian gunners drop shells among their own men. The artillery support was so inaccurate that McCay was eventually forced to direct his gunners to increase their range by 500 yards which meant that the rounds then fell beyond and behind the advancing Germans. The accurate German artillery, however, was devastating the occupied trenches. By 9.40 pm, a report was received at brigade headquarters advising 'front line cannot be held unless reinforcements are sent. Enemy machine gunners are creeping up. No star shells. The artillery is not giving support. Sandbags required in thousands. Men bringing sandbags are being wounded in the back. Water urgently required.'

The 32nd Battalion's report was an accurate reflection of the position facing all the Australian defenders by this time. The need for sandbags to fill gaps in the rear of the old German trenches was so acute that, in several locations, the Australians resorted to plugging holes with the bodies of dead Germans. The commander of the 8th Brigade, Brigadier E. Tivey, agreed to send reinforcements from his brigade

163

reserve, unaware that they had already been sent forward as carrying parties and the survivors absorbed into the defence. The 29th Battalion remained uncommitted but, given its role as the divisional reserve, in theory its release could only be sanctioned by the Divisional Commander. In desperation, Tivey co-opted this reserve without authority and pressed the men into service as carriers and trench-diggers. By 9.30 pm, there were no reinforcements to send nor were there any spare troops left to form carrying parties. Apart from isolated deliveries by men diverted from other tasks, the 8th Brigade had to make do with its current stock of supplies and ammunition.

Enemy bombing was making continued tenure of the *Kastenweg* difficult and parties of defenders were being forced to move out of the trench into shell holes to continue to defend the flank. One resourceful Australian officer brought forward two Lewis guns which, from this exposed position, helped repel this first counter-attack. Somewhat surprisingly, the German accounts mention British artillery fire as part of the reason for their temporary setback. This first counter-attack had not contacted the defenders in the forward defensive lines who comprised part of the 32nd Battalion and the survivors of the 31st. Mixed in with both battalions were troops from the 30th Battalion, the supporting wave, and men from the 29th who had come forward as carriers and remained.

Undeterred by their initial setback, the Bavarians prepared to launch another attack. At first, the Australians feared this would come through No Man's Land from the left and effectively isolate the entire brigade. To their relief, they quickly discovered that the attacks comprised assaults by isolated groups of bombers targeting the men trying to extend the communication trench across to the old German front line. But more substantial counter-attack forces were assembling around Delangré Farm. The survivors of the 8th Brigade would soon be facing the fresh troops of the *Bavarian 14th Brigade* whose two regiments had been reinforced by the divisional reserve.

At 2.15 am, escalating German artillery fire announced the renewed counter-attack on the left flank of the 8th Brigade's position. British artillery attempts to break up the attack by shelling Delangré Farm failed. This time, the first contact occurred on the right of the position, the attackers penetrating the large gap between the 8th and 14th Brigade positions. The right wing of the brigade, consisting mainly of outposts formed by the 31st Battalion, was driven back from its forward position into the old German front line. Eventually, the Germans drove the remnants of the 31st out of the old front line and advanced along the line towards the east. With insufficient men to hold the blocks in the trenches, the defenders eventually withdrew into No Man's Land and back to their original trenches. The Germans, advancing cautiously but with great skill and determination, eventually joined up with the troops who had come westward from the *Kastenweg* and the front-line trenches flanking the captured trenches. Although at first unaware of this development, the remaining Australian defenders were now cut off from all communication with the rear.

On the left flank, the defeat of the earlier counter-attacks had granted the defenders time to reorganise the defences, although they were still subjected to almost continuous bombing and artillery attack. The release of the 29th from reserve allowed some strengthening of the flank protection. The company of the 32nd holding both the northern end of the *Kastenweg* trench and manning the blocks on the flank trenches was able to close up into the *Kastenweg* while the company from the 29th took over the flank protection role. This changeover, affected after midnight, was barely completed when the 32nd defenders heard the sounds of bombing to their rear. At 3.15 am they discovered that the Germans had advanced from the flank trenches and driven the 29th defenders back into No Man's Land. The 150 remaining 32nd troops were now completely cut off. Their only hope was a mad charge back through the attacking enemy in an attempt to regain their own lines. At 3.45 the survivors charged. Fighting hand-to-hand, they punched their way through into No Man's Land and some managed to make it back to their own lines. Other small isolated pockets, many of them men from machine-gun posts, saw what was happening and also began their own attempts to escape. By the time the command conference began at 5.00 am, the survivors of the 8th Brigade were back in their lines and the Germans were again in control of their former positions. With the retreat of the 8th, the position of the 14th Brigade was immediately rendered untenable. The battle was over.

# CHAPTER SEVEN
# CONCLUSIONS

Could the attack at Fromelles have succeeded? Most critics of the decision to launch the attack hold steadfastly to the view that it could not. They point to post-war correspondence between the Official Historians of Australia and Great Britain and to War Office assessments that reach the same conclusion. There is an almost conspiratorial unanimity in seeking to shift full blame for the disaster onto one or two of its architects. However, the rank smell of scapegoating becomes more pronounced when the criticisms are analysed in detail.

The first problem in examining this question is to decide how to define 'success' in terms of this battle. The stated purpose of the attack as expressed in XI Corps Order 100 was to pin the enemy in place and prevent the transfer of unengaged German troops south to the Somme. Having captured a copy of Haking's plan, in which it was emphasised that this was a feint, the Germans would have understood that the British were not planning a second offensive in the area and were therefore free to transfer more reinforcements if necessary. Whether this would have been the case had the attack seized even its limited objectives is more problematic. At this stage, Falkenhayn's orders directing the immediate recapture of lost territory were still in force and the Germans would have been required to conduct expensive counter-attacks to regain their lost ground. As the Somme experience demonstrated, most German losses were incurred during these counter-attacks. Recent evidence now suggests, however, that the Germans *were* concerned about the possibility of another attack and retained sufficient troops in the Lille area to counter this. In terms of that aim, therefore, the battle succeeded.

Could the British attack have succeeded in capturing its limited objectives? The evidence from the Somme, particularly that of the 14 July attack, suggests that it could have, had certain prerequisites been met. What Haking proposed was not vastly different from the 'bite and hold' tactics being developed by Plumer and other commanders. Commanders on both sides were quickly discovering that attacks with limited objectives could be successful. They were never going to win the war, but they could recapture territory. The limited objectives set by Haking's Order 100 were realistic if all parts of the plan worked. His attack was unsuccessful because the component elements failed.

A typical German pill box in the German line on the summit of Fromelles Ridge. From this and adjacent positions devastating fire was poured onto the troops of the 5th Australian Division in the abortive Battle of Fromelles on 19 July 1916.
AWM E03967

Simple success or failure is not necessarily an accurate indicator of either the adequacy of the plan or the competence of the planners. World War One is replete with attacks that, on all objective analysis, should have failed, but succeeded or vice versa. Examples include Australian successes such as the 2nd Division attack at Mont St Quentin and the taking of the St Quentin Canal. The successful attack on Vimy Ridge by the Canadians is another. However, the ability to predict an outcome prior to the attack is not an option open to those who plan and conduct it. In this war, commanders and their staffs could only plan on the basis of the information available at the time.

The causes of the failure of the Battle of Fromelles were complex and numerous. The obvious and critical causes were the haste in preparation, which did not allow sufficient time for reconnaissance or logistic build-up; the failure of the intelligence system both in gaining only a partial understanding of the enemy defences and in misidentifying objects in the enemy lines as objectives for the attack; and, most importantly, the failure of the artillery to fulfil its mission. The artillery failure is arguably matched only in consequence by the lack of security that signalled the enemy that an attack was planned. The failure of the communication systems was also a major problem, especially during the battle. Through the lack of timely information, no commander at any level could intervene to compensate for developments as the battle progressed. Inadequate communication contributed to planning mistakes, command paralysis and battlefield confusion.

The body of an Australian soldier killed in the German second line which was held throughout the night by the 5th Australian Division during the Battle of Fromelles from 19 to 20 July 1916. The photograph was taken on the morning of 20 July after the Germans re-occupied their trenches. AWM A01566

The confusion caused by the 'on again, off again' decision process in the lead-up to the attack is frequently cited as among the more contentious reasons for the failure of the attack. There is no question that it was not a smooth operational process; but given what was prompting it, could it ever have been so? The whole proposal was a reaction to German moves and the requirement for the battle hung on interpretations of German actions. To achieve the desired result, the decision was always going to be a last-minute one. Even accepting that the decision process was flawed, it is still difficult to attach any specific outcome to this problem. Perhaps the lack of time to accumulate stores, which meant that assault troops were exhausted trying to establish stores and ammunition dumps adequate to the task when they should have been resting is one possible outcome. While the assault troops were undoubtedly fatigued, the two-day respite provided by the weather had enabled most to rest. It is also difficult to identify any critical failing at the operational level. Coordination occurred as planned. Supplies came forward into the rear zones and all the combat support functions were delivered (however imperfectly in the case of the artillery). And so they should have been. After two years of war, most planning staffs could cope with last-minute changes in the timing of attacks. After all, only days later, a full attack by Fourth Army on the Somme would have to and did accommodate the last-minute demand by the Australian 1st Division for an extension of time as it wasn't ready to attack Pozieres on the date scheduled.

While Haking does not deserve the degree of opprobrium to which he has been subjected, he does deserve criticism for his handling of aspects of the battle. Having decided to proceed with the attack he should never have permitted the movement of troops and supplies in daylight, thereby guaranteeing that preparations would be observed by the enemy. Recognising the inadequacy of his artillery, he should have paid more attention to the assessment of its effect. However, his decisions were informed by the advice of his experts and they were telling him that his guns were doing the job. It is probably true that Haking wasn't a particularly sensitive man in the modern meaning of that word, and his apparent willingness to put a good 'spin' on the outcome has not endeared him to his critics. All of this pales, however, beside his biggest mistake.

The Sugarloaf was the key to the success of the battle. It dominated both approach lines and its presence enabled the Germans to control No Man's Land. Such an important feature should never have been on the boundary line between two divisions, especially two from different corps. Haking should have given sole and full responsibility for the capture of the Sugarloaf to one division which, in turn, should have assigned a brigade to take it. Both it and the Wick salient were recognised as dominating the battlefield yet the artillery program was not monitored to the degree necessary to ensure the destruction of these positions. For this, as Corps Commander, Haking cannot escape responsibility.

The one theme that emerges from an examination of any of the causes of this failure is that inexperienced and untrained troops cannot be expected to accomplish the same tasks as battle-hardened veterans. The consequence of using untrained gunners has been examined, but it should be noted that inexperience also contributed to the infantry failures. Apart from such obvious errors as throwing grenades without removing the pins, the lack of tactical skill meant that small groups of men, particularly when leaderless, did not know how to secure positions, operate in the confusion of battle or conduct basic minor tactics. The Germans excelled at trench-fighting, but the inexperienced British and Australians perhaps made them appear better than they really were.

In the rush to criticise Haking, another factor is frequently overlooked. He was facing an effective, experienced enemy. The Bavarians had been defending the area for many months and were intimately familiar with the terrain. They could move about at night with confidence. They had studied the terrain and plotted all the approach paths, the dead ground and set up killing grounds for their machine-gunners. Their soldiers had demonstrated resolution in defence and could react quickly when setbacks occurred. In this, they were not much different from the German defenders all along the line. The difference was that Allied artillery was unable to prevent them exploiting their advantages.

The final factor to be considered is luck. According to one argument, generals make their own luck — perhaps this is so. However, they cannot make their own weather. Haking faced a dilemma: BEF HQ determined the timetable for his attack and bad weather interrupted his preparations. In adverse conditions his aircraft and balloon spotters could not range his guns or spot enemy artillery positions; they could not provide him with current photographs of the enemy positions; nor could they monitor the movement of troops on the ground. Rain turned the ditches into obstacles and the soil into mud. The dampness made the already unreliable artillery fuses even more prone to failure. It must have appeared to Haking that even the elements favoured the Germans.

Australian prisoners of war arriving at a German collecting station on the morning of 20 July following the Battle of Fromelles. The German officer, second from the right with his hand on his chest gave this photo and others to Captain C. Mills of the 31st Battalion in Berlin following the Armistice. AWM A01546

# FROMELLES NINETY-FOUR YEARS ON
## EPILOGUE

On a cold Saturday, 30 January 2010, a burial party comprising soldiers from both Britain and Australia reburied with full military honours the remains of a soldier killed during the Battle of Fromelles. The body had been recovered by the Germans and buried with 249 of his colleagues in a series of pits near a wood now known as Pheasant Wood and then forgotten. The story of the search for and recovery of these missing soldiers captured the public imagination, particularly in Australia. The discovery was due almost entirely to a small group of enthusiastic amateur historians in Australia. The recovery operation was mounted by the armies of both countries who took responsibility for recovering and honouring their war dead.

Reinterment of one of the recovered dead
from the Battle of Fromelles, February 2010.
(Australian Army photograph)

## Background to the Discovery

The possibility that the remains of Australian soldiers might lie buried in an area just outside the small northern French village of Fromelles was first suggested to the Australian Army by a school teacher from Victoria, Lambis Englezos, in 2001. Englezos and two colleagues, one of whom was an Army Reserve officer, were convinced that there were unrecovered remains of Australian soldiers at Fromelles, and Englezos approached the Army asking for some form of marker to be placed at the site. How he and his colleagues discovered the existence of the remains is a long and fascinating story, better told elsewhere. Englezos also became something of a crusader on the subject of the Fromelles missing and recruited others to his cause. However, he was less successful in convincing the Army that remains were present at the site or that the Army should investigate his claims.

Lambis Englezos discussing the recovery with a visiting group.
(Australian Army photograph)

There were two reasons for this. The first was that, in 1922, all the victorious governments had agreed that further active searching for war dead should cease. This was partially motivated by financial reasons — it was proving very expensive to retain graves recovery personnel in Europe. But the governments were also motivated by the desire to allow French and Belgian civilians in the battle zones to re-establish some semblance of a normal life. Constant digging for missing soldiers and lost graves was disrupting attempts to build new infrastructure and establish new farms. The second reason the Army was cool in its reaction to Englezos's claim was that the Army Historian had received many such claims previously from individuals insisting that they knew where missing Australians were buried. On investigation, the claims were invariably found to be misguided. Usually, there was evidence in the available records which pointed to where the missing were buried and, for the remainder, the records contained compelling reasons as to why remains would not be where claimed. Englezos understood this scepticism and recognised the need to produce a robust case based on irrefutable evidence. He and his colleagues set about assembling such a case.

The Army also faced something of dilemma. Under existing policy, there could be no speculative searching for remains. Should remains be discovered, however, there were well-established procedures for recovering, identifying and, if they proved to be Commonwealth war dead, reinterring them in a suitable Commonwealth War Graves Commission (CWGC) cemetery. Owing to this long-standing policy, there were no established procedures to instigate a speculative search, irrespective of how compelling the evidence. However, recognition within the Army that this policy required amendment to cover compelling cases was matched by growing political and public pressure to at least examine the evidence. The Army History Unit proposed the convening of an expert panel to examine the evidence presented by Englezos and his colleagues, noting that, should the evidence be sound, the Army would then be obliged to act on the panel's recommendation.

In a major change of policy, the then Chief of Army agreed that, should the panel recommend further investigation, the Army would implement this recommendation. Accordingly, a panel comprising several of Australia's leading military historians, technical experts on aerial photo interpretation, senior Army and Office of Australian War Graves staff, and chaired by the Army Historian, was convened to hear Englezos's case. Following the first hearing, the panel reported that, while the evidence was valid, it lacked sufficient detail to warrant action by the Army. Significantly, however, the panel did invite Englezos to conduct more research. It also tasked the Army with further research, including requesting the German authorities to examine their archival material for any documents relevant to the claimed burials. Following the collection of more evidence by Englezos and his colleagues and by the Army, the panel met twice more, each time recommending further investigation including, after the third meeting, a physical examination of the site.

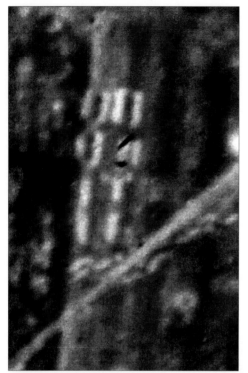

*Left:* An aerial reconnaissance photo of the grave site during July 1916, clearly showing eight open pits, in two rows of four.
*Below*: This photograph is of the same site in 1918, showing five of the eight pits now filled in. Photo courtesy of the AWM.

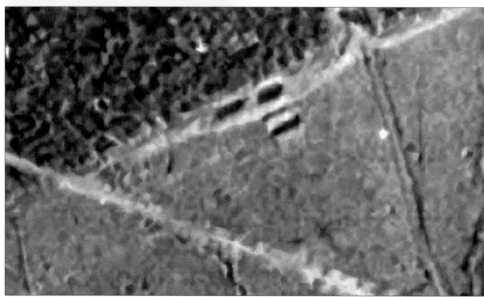

The first archaeological examination of the site occurred in 2007. On the advice of a British expert from the Imperial War Museum, Nigel Steel, the Army contracted a specialist battlefield archaeology group from the University of Glasgow — the Glasgow University Archaeological Research Division (GUARD) — to undertake a limited survey of the alleged burial site. The purpose of the investigation was to determine whether the pits that had been observed in wartime aerial photographs of the site could be located and their characteristics (width, length, depth, condition etc.) established. The team was also tasked with determining whether there was sufficient archaeological evidence present to support a more detailed examination of the site. The 2007 GUARD report was a carefully constructed and robust consideration of all the available evidence at the site. Based on determining factors including battlefield debris scatter, soil chemistry and radar profiles, GUARD was convinced the pits remained intact. On this assessment, the Australian Army decided a full investigation was warranted.

## The Proof Stage

The supporting archival research had also strengthened the probability that, should remains still be present, they could include both British and Australian soldiers. For this reason, a new group was established to oversee the investigation and, should remains be discovered, manage the post-discovery process. The new group, the Fromelles Evaluation Group (FEG), comprised representatives from the Australian and British governments and was chaired by the CWGC. While the CWGC was not in the business of searching for remains, it was, by international treaty, the organisation responsible for all dealings with British Empire war dead in France and Belgium. Clearly, this was the appropriate organisation to coordinate the remaining phases of the investigation and manage any discoveries. Given its treaty status, the CWGC also had better liaison links with the relevant French authorities, as well as personnel *in situ* to manage day-to-day issues. The Australian Army, however, provided the bulk of the resources, both human and financial, required to conduct this phase. With the administrative arrangements in place, it merely remained to discover whether or not the Pheasant Wood site contained the remains of missing war dead.

On 26 May 2008, a large group of impressively qualified people arrived to commence the final phase of the investigation of the site. Managing expectations both on the site (the press was present in overwhelming numbers) and among the interested public was one of the major tasks confronting the Army team.

Two members of the Army team – Team leader Major General Mike O'Brien and Australian Embassy staff interpreter Mr Sam Rossato at the commemoration ceremony at the end of the proof stage.
(Australian Army photograph)

Based on its previous work and the established competence of the team, GUARD was again tasked with conducting the investigation. The team leader was Dr Tony Pollard with Dr Iain Banks as the project director for GUARD. The excavation itself was conducted by three teams comprising one very experienced forensic anthropologist or archaeologist as team leader plus specialist assistance. One of the teams was headed by an Australian, Gaille MacKinnon, who was also the project anthropologist. The GUARD team was a truly international group, with a French survey team and other specialists from Spain and the UK. No account of the onsite activity would be complete without mention of the local CWGC staff member and expert on the battle, Martial Delebarre OAM. Martial knows the battlefield better than any person alive and has been exploring it and recovering items from it for many years.

The investigation plan involved making a small excavation across each pit and digging down to the point identified by the scientific survey as the bottom of the pit. Team members were a little concerned about pits 6, 7 and 8 as these were not filled in until the end of the war and could have been used for the dumping of wartime rubbish and debris. Hitting an unexploded shell with the back-hoe was an alarming prospect.

Martial Delebarre with an indispensable tool – a pump to remove the enormous amount of water that flooded the site. In the background is the exposed Pit 8. (Australian Army photograph)

Dr Tony Pollard providing a progress report on the site. *From left*: Roger Lee, Australian Army historian, Major General Mike O'Brien, Dr Pollard, Mr Peter Barton, contract historian and archive researcher for the Australian Army, Major General Paul Stevens (Ret'd), Director Office of Australian War Graves, a French Official and the Mayor of Fromelles, M. Hubert Huchette. (Australian Army photograph)

The location of the pits, already identified through aerial photography and the previous site investigation, was marked out carefully. There were eight pits altogether, in two rows of four. They ran parallel with the southern edge of Pheasant Wood.

Work started officially on Monday, 26 May 2008. The plan was to make a cut of around two metres wide across each pit and dig down to the pit base. The overburden was lifted very carefully by back-hoe, after which all digging proceeded by hand, with team members employing everything from trowels to plastic picks the size of a toothpick. Sometimes exploratory holes called 'sondages' were dug using shovels.

Day one began with the excavator cutting two long trenches across each pair of pits to establish their exact location and their proximity to one another. The cuts were also used to examine the soil profile. All the spoil was subjected to close scrutiny, including a careful search by metal detector and meticulous examination by hand.

A view of a sondage. Clearly visible in this excavation is the layer of thick lime (the white substance) used by the Germans to cover the bodies once they were laid out in the pit. Also visible is the thick, heavy and virtually impervious grey Ypresian clay. (Australian Army photograph)

Two members of the GUARD team, Dr Olivia Lelong and Cecily Cropper, deep in a pit. The yellow drum in the background is for the collection of contaminated water recovered from the pits. (Australian Army photograph)

By the end of the first day, the cuts had found the top of each of the pits. They were amazingly clear. Looking down on them from the end of the hole, the cut marks made by the Bavarian soldiers' shovels in 1916 were easily discernible. But no human remains were found.

On day two the teams began to make rapid progress. Sondages were dug in each of the pits of interest (1 to 5) and, by mid-afternoon, the first remains had been discovered. This generated considerable emotion among all those present. Having found the remains, the rest of the time was dedicated to determining how many sets of remains were present. This was essential information for planning the next stage. It was a long, laborious process and occupied practically all the allocated time for the investigation. Each pit was systematically examined and the investigation excavation was taken to the bottom of each pit. Under the agreement with French authorities, the team was not permitted to remove any remains and the archaeologists had to work around them. As many lay on top of one another, this was a difficult and trying task. When the mud was taken into account — and mud was the defining physical factor on the site — it was an extraordinary effort by the team. Team members often lay across

179

a board and worked head down, spending hours below ground in the cramped, filthy and malodorous pits without complaint. The relatively well preserved state of the remains, including those exhibiting significant battle trauma, generated much surprise and considerable scientific interest.

Water was a constant problem during this phase of the investigation. Dr Iain Banks, Martial Delebarre and Dr Steve Litherland turn to mechanical means to remove the inundation from Pit 3. (Australian Army photograph)

Apart from the remains themselves, a number of other objects were uncovered. Buckles and buttons from both Australian and British pattern uniforms helped establish likely nationalities of the remains. A number of small objects were also retrieved such as standard British General Service buttons, eyelets from both British and German ground sheets, shrapnel balls of both sizes, and some major objects such as a set of 1908 pattern webbing, complete with .303 rounds *in situ*. While the canvas on the webbing had largely decayed, the buckles, loops and strap-ends were all in their original locations. One surprising discovery was the remains of a matchbox — John Bull Safety Matches — so well preserved that the name on the box and its colour were still vividly apparent.

A recovered, remarkably well preserved Australian 'Rising Sun' badge.
(Australian Army photogaph)

Madame Demassiet in discussion with the Australian and British Army
representatives at the commemoration ceremony.
(Australian Army photograph)

It took just on two weeks to investigate the site and then return it to its previous state. The planned time-frame was met, despite the weather and other interruptions. On the last day, an intensely moving ceremony was held during which the owner of the land, a remarkable elderly French lady, Madame Demassiet, donated the site to the memory of the dead.

## Recovery

With the confirmation of the presence of remains, both governments moved quickly to initiate recovery and reinterment. The Fromelles Evaluation Group changed both role and title to become the Fromelles Management Board (FMB). The FMB was established to coordinate the efforts on behalf of both governments and the CWGC. The Australian Army created a full-time specialised project team to assist in the recovery, reinterment, identification and commemoration of the Pheasant Wood soldiers. One of the FMB's first actions was to issue a worldwide Request for Tender, under the authority of the CWGC, inviting qualified organisations to tender for the recovery operation.

The Deputy Chief of the Australian Army, Major General Paul Symon, presents a commendation to Mr David Richardson of the CWGC for his contribution to the recovery operation.
(Australian Army photograph)

The Australian Army project team managing the recovery operations.
From left to right: Lieutenant Colonel James Brownlie, Major General
Mike O'Brien and Major Jason Kerr. Behind the camera was the team's
Public Affairs Officer, Ms Chloe Wootten.
(Australian Army photograph)

Recovery work under way in Pit (now called Grave) 1.
(Australian Army photograph)

Oxford Archaeology (not part of Oxford University) won the tender for the full excavation and, between 5 May and 30 September 2009, meticulously recovered the 250 men and associated artefacts from the site. A temporary onsite mortuary and processing laboratory was established to document every detail of the operation and ensure the best chances of identification. The archaeological and anthropological teams worked through the height of the French summer in head-to-toe Tyvek suits to avoid contamination of DNA. The professionalism of this team laid the foundation for identification efforts through anthropological analysis to match against enlistment and medical records.

Efforts to identify the remains using a range of historical, archaeological and scientific techniques commenced following the recovery operation and will continue until all prospects of identification have been exhausted. In Australia, over 2,200 relatives of soldiers who may be among those at Pheasant Wood have registered with the project in the hope of helping to identify the men.

Oxford's work provided the basis for another layer of scientific analysis. LGC Forensics took samples from each set of remains in the hope of matching them against samples taken from living relatives. Not all relatives are genetically suitable for the testing and some families have been unable to find relatives who can provide the necessary DNA. LGC, ably assisted by Orchid Cellmark, were able to extract viable DNA from all the remains, so there is still hope that many of the men will eventually be identified. Over 800 samples were taken from living relatives prior to the 2010 identification boards and, with ninety-four soldiers now named, it appears the work to name the remainder has only just begun.

When all the historical and scientific evidence was assembled, a Joint Identification Board (JIB) was convened to examine the evidence and provide an independent assessment of the case. No remains would be considered identified unless the JIB was convinced by supporting arguments. The first meeting of the JIB considered historical accounts, artefacts recovered with the remains, anthropological analysis of the remains against enlistment records and DNA evidence from samples matched with living relatives of the missing. This resulted in the naming of ninety-four Australian soldiers and the identification of a further 111 as Australian. Three of the bodies were identified as British soldiers, leaving forty-two as unknown.

Tyvek suits — not the most comfortable of garments in summer temperatures.
(Australian Army photograph)

CWGC expert advice that the burial site itself was unsuited to the construction of a war cemetery led to the establishment of a new cemetery across the road from the village church within sight of the burial pits.

Working on the new cemetery at Fromelles.
(Australian Army photograph)

Location of the new cemetery in relation to the discovery site and the village of Fromelles. (Australian Army photograph)

*Above*: Aerial view of the new cemetery. (Australian Army Photograph)

*Left*: A headstone in the new cemetery. (Australian Army photograph)

All the remains were recovered by the start of September 2009 and they were all, with a single exception, reinterred in the new cemetery throughout January and February 2010. Each body was given an individual military burial by serving members of the Australian Army, the 1st Battalion, Royal Regiment of Fusiliers, and the 4th Battalion, The Rifles. This new cemetery will be dedicated and officially opened at a major ceremony on the 94th anniversary of the Battle of Fromelles on 19 July 2010.

Further identifications through DNA sampling of living relatives may be made as more families come forward.

# BIOGRAPHIES

## GENERAL ERICH GEORG ANTON SEBASTIAN VON FALKENHAYN

In 1916, the man responsible for the conduct of all German military operations was German Commander-in-Chief General of Infantry Erich Georg Anton Sebastian von Falkenhayn. While his position was in some ways comparable to his British and French counterparts Haig and Joffre, as Chief of the Imperial German General Staff and principal military adviser to the Kaiser, Falkenhayn's military responsibilities covered all the operational theatres in which German troops were fighting.

Falkenhayn was born in Burg Belchau near Graudenz in West Prussia on 11 November 1861 to aristocratic but impoverished parents. He joined the infantry after graduating from cadet school, eventually proceeding to the *Kriegsacademie* to be trained as a staff officer.

Between 1896 and 1903, Falkenhayn served in China and saw action during the Boxer Rebellion where his reports of that bloody insurrection attracted the attention of the Kaiser. On his return to Germany, Falkenhayn rose steadily through the ranks of the German General Staff and was promoted lieutenant general just prior to the war. In 1913 he was appointed Prussian Minister for War and exercised considerable influence over the Kaiser during the lead-up to the war. The German defeat at the Battle of the Marne and the mental breakdown of the German commander, von Moltke, saw Falkenhayn succeed him as Chief of Staff in September 1914, despite being junior in rank to all the other army and corps commanders in the German Army. He retained his political appointment as Minister for State and Minister for War until 20 January 1915 when, formally relieved of his political responsibilities, he was promoted General of Infantry.

As Chief of Staff, Falkenhayn had to balance the competing demands of the Western and Eastern Fronts. His understanding of Germany's strategic situation encouraged him to give maximum priority to the military effort on the Western Front in an attempt to knock France out of the war. This brought him into conflict with other senior German officers such as Hindenburg and German politicians such as the German Chancellor, Bethmann-Hollweg. His emphasis on the Western Front eventually culminated in the Verdun operation, the failure of which led to his dismissal on 29 August 1916. The Kaiser also blamed Falkenhayn's western-focused strategy for the entry of Rumania into the war on the Allied side.

Although removed from his position as *de facto* Chief of Staff, Falkenhayn retained his rank and was given command of Ninth Army, somewhat ironically, on the Rumanian Front. His forces defeated the Rumanians at the Battle of the Red Tower Pass on 30 September 1916 and his troops entered Bucharest on 6 December 1916, knocking Rumania out of the war.

Following this success, Falkenhayn was sent to Turkey in early 1917 to command the Ottoman Forces in Palestine, but under the overall command of the German General Liman von Sanders. There, he faced the British forces (including several Australian mounted divisions) of General Allenby. His Ottoman troops proved unable to resist the relentless British advance and were defeated at Gaza in October 1917 and driven from Jerusalem in December the same year. He was relieved of his command in February 1918 and returned to Germany where he retired from the military. Falkenhayn died near Potsdam on 8 April 1922.

## GENERAL ALEXEI ALEKSEEVICH BRUSILOV

Whether deserved or not, General Brusilov is one of the few Russian generals to emerge from the war with a positive reputation. His promoters extol his military skills as an innovator and developer of new offensive tactics. He is remembered as an unusual Russian commander who was concerned about his men and tried to minimise unnecessary casualties. He fought successfully for both the Romanovs and the Bolsheviks.

Brusilov was born in Tiflis, in Georgia, on 19 March 1853. His father was a lieutenant general in the Imperial Russian Army but died when Alexei was still young. Alexei was raised by his uncle, a military engineer. In 1867 he was accepted into the Corps of Pages, a prestigious military educational establishment. On graduating in 1872, he was commissioned into the cavalry, the 15th Tver Dragoons, and had his first operational experience with this regiment in the Russo–Turkish War of 1877–78, where he demonstrated considerable bravery and early leadership promise. An accomplished horseman, Brusilov was accepted into the Officer Cavalry School in 1881 which further advanced his career prospects. By 1906 he had risen to the rank of general. In the eight years prior to the outbreak of World War One, Brusilov commanded the 2nd Guard Cavalry Division and the 12th and 14th Corps, as well as holding senior training appointments. These commands provided excellent preparation for the challenges he was soon to face.

Brusilov was on holiday in Germany when war broke out and was fortunate to escape to Russia. His initial wartime command, the 8th Army, was on the left or southern flank of the Eastern Front and he found himself fighting the Austro-Hungarians in Galicia. It was during this early fighting that Brusilov refined the ideas that were to stand him in good stead in 1916. However, it could also be argued that the lacklustre soldiers and poor leadership of the Austro-Hungarians led Brusilov to develop tactical concepts that would have failed badly if used against German troops.

In March 1916, Brusilov was appointed Commander-in-Chief of the South West Front ('front' is roughly equivalent to a field army in Western parlance). His initial task was to launch a diversionary attack, but he considered his army to be capable of much more and he persuaded the Russian High Command to allow him to launch a full-scale attack. On 22 May 1916 a heavy preparatory artillery barrage began and, on 4 June, the attack that bears his name commenced. An initial period of spectacular success was followed by a slowing of the advance as supplies and reinforcements dwindled and the logistic effort involved in supplying such a large army in an area with little transport infrastructure became insurmountable. The offensive finally halted on 20 September and, within a year, most of the area captured by Brusilov was back in enemy hands.

Growing internal political instability began to affect the Russian Army and, in March 1917, the autocratic government of the Tsar was replaced by a Provisional Government under Alexander Kerensky. Brusilov was appointed Supreme Commander-in-Chief of the Russian Army and immediately launched a new offensive — known as the Kerensky Offensive — on 1 July 1917. This offensive, which employed thirty-one divisions of the new 'Red Army', exhibited the usual pattern of Russian attacks in this war: a good start followed by rapid failure. In this case, poor morale and the inevitable supply difficulties slowed the attacks even before German reinforcements arrived to halt them completely. Brusilov paid the price for failure and was replaced by General Lavr Kornilov. However, the damage done to the Army by this final offensive proved fatal and Russian political and military cohesion collapsed. The Bolsheviks came to power in October 1917 and, by March 1918, had concluded a peace treaty with the Germans.

Brusilov remained aloof from politics for the early years of the Bolshevik period but, when Poland went to war with Russia in April 1920, he offered his services and was instrumental in bringing over 14,000 former Tsarist officers back into Russian military service. Later, during the savage fighting in Crimea, he made a similar call to officers of the White Russian forces to return. Unfortunately, he was betrayed by his communist leaders who ignored the promised amnesty and had many of those who returned to the Army killed.

Despite this betrayal of his trust, Brusilov remained in the Red Army until 1924, ending his career as Inspector of Cavalry. He died in Moscow two years later on 17 March 1926.

## FIELD MARSHAL SIR DOUGLAS HAIG

Sir Douglas Haig, commander of the BEF for the last half of the Great War, remains a controversial figure in the bulk of English language studies of that war. Everything about the man — from his personality to his military competence — has been analysed and scrutinised to such an extent that it is difficult to adopt a fresh perspective on Haig. In popular culture he is either perceived as a caricature of cold indifference or as the epitome of bone-headed stupidity. Judgements and criticisms of the man have been repeated so often that they have built a validity based on repetition rather than evidence. There is no doubt that Douglas Haig made mistakes, but the almost irrevocable public perception of him as a callous incompetent who needlessly sacrificed millions of men is neither fair nor accurate.

While branches of the Haig family came from the socially desirable landed aristocracy, Douglas was fortunate enough to be born into the branch that was wealthy. His father, John Haig, was the head of the Haig and Haig whisky distilling firm and Douglas was thus spared the necessity to work for a living. He was born in Edinburgh on 19 June 1861 but was educated at Clifton College in Bristol. Even then, his school prided itself on its emphasis on science rather than social elitism, although whether this had any influence on the future field marshal is difficult to discern. Haig attended Oxford University from 1880 to 1883, but left before taking his degree so as to gain admission to Sandhurst while he was young enough to qualify for entry. He graduated from Sandhurst in 1884 and joined the 7th (Queen's Own) Hussars. In contrast to later views on his intellectual ability, he graduated at the top of his Sandhurst class, winning the Anson Memorial Sword as Senior Under-Officer and also gaining distinction as an athlete.

During this period — described by one notable military historian as one of the three 'low points' in the history of the British Army — Douglas Haig's career followed the standard pattern of regimental service. He served nine years with the Hussars, primarily in India. Unlike the typical young British officer of the time, however, Haig spent as much time as he could learning his trade and developing his military skills. In 1893 he left the Regiment in India and returned to England to sit the Staff College entrance examination. He failed on his first attempt but succeeded in gaining a place in the 1895 intake. While waiting to enter Staff College at Camberley, Haig visited the Continent, touring Germany at length where he observed military developments and wrote detailed, highly analytical and insightful commentaries based on his observations. He was recognised, even at this early stage, as something of an expert on the German Army.

Haig spent two profitable years at Staff College, deriving perhaps the greatest benefit from the links he established with the men beside whom he would later fight and others he would command. While Camberley had an enormous impact on his military education and skills, he was thirty-six years old and still only a captain when he left at the end of 1897. At this stage in his career, only his intellectual ability suggested his future rise to the highest possible command.

After Staff College, Haig spent five years in the field: first in the Omdurman campaign of 1897–1898, then the Second Boer War of 1899–1902 where he served with distinction. By now, his abilities were being recognised at the highest level and Haig served in a series of important staff positions, including Director of Military Training in 1906 and Chief of Staff of the Indian Army in 1909. Between 1912 and 1914 he was promoted lieutenant general and given the plum command appointment of General Officer Commanding (GOC) Aldershot Command. Of these key appointments, it was probably his time as Director of Military Training, when he worked closely with the Secretary of State for War, Richard Haldane, in reforming the British Army and preparing it to operate on the Continent, that did most to prepare him for his future role.

As GOC Aldershot, Haig helped organise the BEF — in fact, his own command became one of the two initial corps of the BEF. Although Haig and the Commander of the BEF, Sir John French, had previously enjoyed a long and generally amicable relationship, the different style and capabilities of the two men soon generated tensions. While Haig made mistakes in this early fighting, French soon lost the confidence of both his own superiors and, perhaps more critically, his French allies. Apart from his errors in the fighting around Mormal Forest, Haig performed well enough to be promoted full general in November 1914 and was given command when his I Corps expanded to become First Army in December. Concern grew in both Whitehall and in the BEF over French's performance in 1915. The battles of Neuve Chapelle and Second Ypres were followed by the disaster of Loos, after which French's replacement as Commander of the BEF became inevitable. On 10 December, Haig was appointed Commander-in-Chief in French's place.

The new Commander-in-Chief was given two simple directives by the Secretary of State for War: defeat the German Army and liberate occupied France and Belgium. He was also told in no uncertain terms that, while he should cooperate with his French allies, he was not under their command. These factors combined to present Haig with a challenging operational environment. In the forty-four months that he commanded the BEF, he had to reconcile these directions with a government that withheld troop reinforcements at whim for political reasons and tried to place him under command of the French while still expecting him to protect Great Britain's strategic interests in the war. For the simple fact that he delivered victory in spite of the dual problems of a capable enemy and a scheming government at home, Haig's command warrants fair assessment.

Haig's first priority was to build and train his army. Based on the standards of the original BEF, the Kitchener Divisions that now comprised the bulk of the British forces were poorly trained and Haig and his senior commanders were understandably concerned about their readiness for war. However, the German attack at Verdun denied Haig the time he needed to complete his training program and he was forced to commit his partially trained and poorly supported troops to the biggest land operation in British military history, the operation with which he is indelibly associated — the Somme Offensive. Launched on 1 July 1916 and finally ending on 18 November, the enormous loss of men's lives weighed against the small tactical achievements appears to be a major contributor to the popular perception of Haig as incompetent and uncaring. Certainly, Haig's political critics, including the Prime Minister, David Lloyd George, and Winston Churchill, tried to shift any responsibility attributed to them for the carnage of the war onto Haig's shoulders, thus feeding the popular perception and the enduring injustice to Haig's reputation.

Haig was convinced that the only path to victory lay in the destruction of the German Army in the west, and he steadfastly pursued an offensive strategy aimed at achieving this. A major offensive was launched in each of the three years of his command and all had one strategic aim: to break through the German lines and roll up the disintegrating German Army's flanks and rear. Until 1918, the strength of the German defence and the lack of suitable offensive capability denied Haig strategic success. Historians continue to argue whether the huge losses inflicted on his own army, which could be replaced (including by Americans once the United States entered the war) were justified and whether these contributed to eventual victory by inflicting equally heavy losses on the Germans, whose armies could not be replaced.

After successfully repulsing the last German attack of the war in early 1918, Haig's armies launched an offensive in August that year which did not end until Germany was defeated in November. While the casualty rates among the British soldiers in the last few months of the war matched, or at times exceeded, those of the Somme battles as a percentage of those involved, public reaction was not and has never been as critical. Ironically, perhaps, these successful last few months of the war seem almost forgotten by Haig's critics and the public in general. Some of Haig's critics even suggest that the post-August 1918 successes occurred because Haig's generals largely ignored him and conducted their operations independently of GHQ control. The evidence in support of this assessment is unconvincing.

Haig continued to serve after the end of the war and was Commander-in-Chief of the British Home Forces until he retired in 1921. The government recognised his considerable achievements and he was created an earl in 1919 and then Baron Haig of Bemersyde in 1921. In retirement, Haig worked tirelessly for the welfare of the troops he had previously commanded, largely through the Royal British Legion which he helped establish. When he died on Sunday, 29 January 1928, the British nation and the Empire mourned the man later generations have learned to despise.

## GENERAL SIR CHARLES CARMICHAEL MONRO

Charles Carmichael Monro was, somewhat unusually, born at sea on the SS *Maid of Judah* on 15 June 1860. Monro had connections to Australia through his father, Henry Monro, who had emigrated to Australia from Scotland in 1834 and settled on a property near Hotspur in Victoria. The move was unsuccessful and Henry eventually returned to Europe via Argentina, dying in Malaga, Spain, in 1869. His widow, Catherine, second wife and mother of Charles, died in London in 1889. Charles enjoyed the traditional childhood of the privileged classes, educated at Sherborne School and the Royal Military Academy, Sandhurst, before being commissioned into the 2nd Regiment of Foot in 1879. Like many of his contemporaries, he served in the Boer War, filling an appointment as a staff officer and fighting at the Battle of Paardeberg in 1900.

After the war Monro was posted to the School of Musketry at Hythe and promoted colonel in 1903. He remained at the school until 1907 when he was appointed Commander of the 13th Infantry Brigade in Dublin. In 1912 he was posted to command the 2nd London Division and promoted to major general. With the outbreak of war in 1914, Monro took his division — one of the original divisions of the BEF — to France where it played an important part in the retreat from Mons and the first battle of Ypres. In December 1914 he was again promoted and given command of I Corps, which he led during the bloody battles of 1915 at Aubers Ridge, Festubert and Givenchy. He moved briefly to command of III Corps before being despatched to the Mediterranean theatre to relieve Sir Ian Hamilton. It was Monro who, accurately assessing the situation at Gallipoli as unwinnable, recommended to Lord Kitchener that the Allies evacuate the peninsula. (The chief advocate of Gallipoli, Winston Churchill, believed Monro was influenced by his Western Front focus and said of him and his recommendation to withdraw: 'He came, he saw, he capitulated.') The withdrawal from Gallipoli was one of the few military successes of that unhappy campaign and Monro's role in its success is usually overlooked.

Following the end of the Gallipoli campaign, Monro returned to the Western Front to command the British First Army from January 1916. He commanded this army in two major but unsuccessful battles, Vimy Ridge in May and Fromelles in July 1916. In October of that year his time on the Western Front ended. He was promoted general and posted as regional Commander-in-Chief to India, where he served until 1920. He spent the remaining years of the war focusing on the efficiency of the Indian Army, which attained a very high military standard under his guidance.

Following some extended leave, Monro served first as Governor then as Commander of Gibraltar between 1923 and 1928. In 1921 he was created Baronet of Bearcrofts. He died at Westminster on 7 December 1929.

# GENERAL SIR RICHARD CYRIL BYRNE HAKING

Richard Haking, 'Dicky' to his intimates, is probably third on the list of British Commanders most despised by the AIF, after Hubert Gough and Douglas Haig. This is because of one action: his planning and command of the Battle of Fromelles as the Corps Commander, XI Corps. With all the loss and sacrifice that accompanied warfare on the Western Front, it is no mean achievement to earn such animosity based on one brief event. Unfortunately, whether deserved or not, his reputation as an incompetent bully remains almost unassailable in the literature on the war.

Haking was born on 24 January 1862. Most biographies appear uncertain as to the exact details of his birth, asserting that it was 'probably in Halifax and [he was] the son of a clergyman.' He was commissioned into the Hampshire Regiment in 1881.

Given his popular image as an incompetent, it is surprising to discover that he was one of the most educated British officers of his day, serving as a professor at the Staff College and writing two well-received, comprehensive and influential manuals on education and training entitled *Staff Rides and Regimental Tours* and *Company Training*. Like many other military scholars trying to assess the impact of emerging technologies on warfare, Haking made a number of pronouncements on the comparison between materiel and morale that would later contribute to his poor reputation. He was a strong exponent of the view that well-trained and well-motivated troops were the decisive factor in battle. While, from a post-1918 perspective, this was clearly a recipe for mass slaughter, prior to the war it did not seem at all unreasonable. His critics forget that most of the leading military scholars of the day from all the future combatant nations were of the same view that high morale would prevail over base material considerations (Colonel Grandmaison in France, for example, was another noted exponent of the dominance of morale). The experiences of Imperial policing, in which small numbers of well-trained British infantry defeated hordes of irregular tribesmen, were still relatively recent and seemed to sustain such an assessment (although it did require some mental agility to set aside the experience in South Africa which was not nearly as supportive of the theory). While at Staff College, Haking also developed a close relationship with another educated soldier, Douglas Haig.

On the outbreak of war, Haking was given command of the 5th Brigade which he took to France. He fought with the brigade with some distinction until a head wound in September 1914 forced him out of the war for three months. Despite some later accusations, his personal bravery could not be questioned.

Having made a full recovery, Haking returned to the Western Front in December to command the 1st Division until September 1915 when he was promoted to command of XI Corps. His critics have claimed that his promotions were due to Haig's influence, and Haig may certainly have played a part. Equally, however, the tenfold expansion of the British Army created a severe shortage of officers with any experience of commanding divisions or larger. It is difficult to see how Haking could have been overlooked as the vacancies arose.

It was his period of command of XI Corps and its operations around the Aubers Ridge area in 1915 and 1916 that earned him his reputation both as an incompetent commander and as a 'butcher' who cared little for the casualty rate among his own soldiers as he pursued pointless doomed attacks, presumably for his own self-promotion. This reputation drew sustenance from his pre-war views on the efficacy of morale in battle and his frontal attacks against entrenched machine-guns were interpreted as evidence that his thinking was out of touch with the new form of warfare.

After the 1916 operations, XI Corps and Haking moved to Italy to prop up the Italian Army following the disastrous Battle of Caporetto. Haking remained in Italy until March 1918 when he returned to France to face the German March offensives. In both these operations XI Corps and Haking appear to have performed reasonably well although, as usual, casualties were high. He continued to command the corps until the end of the war.

Haking remained in the army after the war, serving with the Armistice Commission, commanding the British Military Mission to Russia in 1919, and British troops in the plebiscite area of East Prussia and Danzig in 1920. He was High Commissioner of the League of Nations in Danzig between 1921 and 1923 and, finally, served as GOC British Troops in Egypt from 1923 to 1927. He retired from the army in 1927 and died on 9 June 1945.

It is doubtful that the reputation of any of World War One generals can ever be salvaged in the public memory. It would be particularly difficult to restore Haking's reputation. However, there is much inconsistency and unfairness in many of the attacks on him. With hindsight, any action can be presented as foolish or pointless. It is only by examining the evidence available to him at the time and questioning in detail what use he made of it that any reasonable judgement can be made.

One of the most common accusations hurled at Haking is that he possessed a fatal attraction to the Aubers Ridge area. Quite possibly he did and just as possibly this attraction had a basis in reasonable military judgement. Aubers Ridge was the key to Lille and a large part of occupied France. Had the British been able to capture the ridge, the German line in northern France would have been seriously compromised. To any military commander, the strategic value of the ground would have been apparent — that the Germans certainly thought so is clear in their efforts to protect it. Similarly, many critics accuse Haking of making pointless attacks against those parts of the German line where the casualty count would be high. None of these critics ever identifies those parts of the line he should have attacked instead. This is because there were no 'soft' parts to the German line.

Finally, many critics accuse Haking of being a 'bully' or use other such pejorative descriptions of him, usually based on the opinions of those who had come into contact with him. These may or may not be accurate judgments. The senior ranks of the British Army (including the AIF) were as riven with jealousy and intrigue as any other organisation and the comments seized on so enthusiastically by Haking's detractors may be equally the views of someone who was a competitor or who had been dismissed by him, of whom Sir James Montagu-Stuart-Wortley is but one example.

# MAJOR GENERAL SIR COLIN JOHN MACKENZIE

Major General Colin Mackenzie is not accorded the same reputation for incompetence in Australia as his immediate commander, Lieutenant General Sir Richard Haking. Within British military history circles, however, Mackenzie's reputation as a battlefield commander is hardly glowing. Having been sacked for bungling one battle early in the war, Mackenzie was barely rehabilitated and back on the Western Front when his new command was given the almost impossible task of capturing the Sugarloaf salient.

Colin John Mackenzie was born on 26 November 1861. He was the eldest son of Major General Colin Mackenzie of the Madras Staff Corps. His Scottish aristocratic heritage would not have been an impediment to advancement so it is interesting that he was commissioned into the Bedfordshire Regiment in January 1881. He served with the Bedfordshires for sixteen months before transferring to the Seaforth Highlanders.

Like most officers of the time, he spent the next twenty years of his military career soldiering on the Empire's outposts, from Burma to Waziristan and Gilgit to South Africa. Although older than was usual for entry, his experience and record of service enabled him to attend Staff College, and he graduated as a full colonel. Following Staff College, he served in a series of staff appointments, including a number of senior divisional staff positions. Although he had never commanded a battalion, he was given command of the 4th Brigade in March 1907. Another brigade command followed before he was appointed to the challenging position of Chief of the General Staff in Canada. He eventually departed Canada having fallen out with the Canadian Minister of Militia and Defence, Sam Hughes, over several issues, including the unsuitability of the Ross Rifle, one of Hughes' pet projects. Mackenzie was later vindicated when the Ross Rifle was proven unsuited to battlefield conditions in 1915.

Returning home in March 1914, Mackenzie was given command of the Highland Division, a Territorial Force division, until war broke out and he was appointed to command the 3rd Division in France. His command lasted only two weeks before he was 'invalided' home — or, more correctly, sacked, for failures in an attack at La Bassée. Surprisingly, instead of being retired, he was given command of a division in Scotland and then moved to an important staff job — Director of Staff Duties at the War Office. Mackenzie probably benefited both from being in the system and visible and from the fact that the BEF Commander who had him invalided out had subsequently been sacked. This was enough for Mackenzie to be rehabilitated. In May 1916, he secured another fighting command when given the 61st (2nd South Midland) Division. Within two months, he took this under-strength and poorly prepared division into battle at Fromelles. Although Fromelles was a disaster for the 61st, Mackenzie remained in command until April 1918. A sniper's bullet through the cheek was slow to heal and he was invalided home a second time. He recovered too late to rejoin the fighting, finishing his army career as Inspector of Infantry.

Major General Mackenzie retired from the Army on 1 April 1920. In retirement he occupied the honorary position of Colonel of the Seaforth Highlanders. He died on 7 July 1956, aged ninety-four.

# LIEUTENANT GENERAL SIR JAMES WHITESIDE MCCAY

Lieutenant General Sir James Whiteside McCay commanded the 5th Australian Division at the Battle of Fromelles. Until the battle, his military reputation was sound, and his personal bravery unquestionable. McCay was never popular with the troops under his command, his contemporaries or his staff, but he was nonetheless well regarded as a competent trainer of soldiers with a strong focus on discipline. The Battle of Fromelles marked the climax of his career. His alleged contribution to the failure of the attack, both genuine and perceived, led eventually to his sideways move to an administrative command in England in January 1917. He ended the war as the senior Australian general in England, with responsibility for training new replacements and reinforcements on Salisbury Plain.

McCay (who as a youth signed his name M'Cay) was born on 21 December 1864 at Ballynure, Antrim, Ireland. He was the eldest of ten children of the Reverend Andrew Ross Boyd McCay, a Presbyterian minister. The family migrated to Australia in 1865 and settled in the Victorian country town of Castlemaine. Initially attending the local state school, McCay won a scholarship to Scotch College, Melbourne, at the age of twelve, graduating dux of the school the following year. He attended Melbourne University, where he displayed a flair for classics and mathematics but did not complete his degree. He also learned several European languages. He began his working life as a teacher — he bought the grammar school in Castlemaine and installed himself as headmaster in 1885 — and revealed an interesting mixture of traits. A firm disciplinarian who frequently used physical punishment, he was also and unusually a strong advocate for the education of women. He completed his degree including the study of law while teaching, which allowed him to leave teaching and set up a practice as a solicitor in Castlemaine in 1897.

Typical of the middle class gentry of his day, McCay was active in the local militia. He was commissioned as a lieutenant in the 4th Battalion of the Victorian Rifles, eventually reaching the rank of lieutenant colonel in 1900. He also began a long career in politics. In 1890 he was elected to the local council and, in 1895, to the Victorian Parliament. Something of a turbulent politician, he lost his seat in 1900 before winning a federal seat in the new Commonwealth Parliament in 1903. His ambition coupled with an ability to alienate people ensured his political career was dynamic. As Minister for Defence in 1905, he demonstrated considerable ability and understanding and played a major role in shaping the new military force of the Commonwealth. A redistribution in 1906, however, saw him lose his lower house seat. An unsuccessful attempt for the Senate was his last foray into politics and he returned to the law and to the militia. Building on his skills and the friendships he had formed as minister, he was promoted colonel in 1907 and given command of the newly formed Australian Intelligence Corps. Under his guidance the corps flourished, becoming active in the staff process. McCay continued his pattern of alienating many of those with whom he dealt, including by 1912, the entire Military Board. The Intelligence Corps was placed under a permanent officer in 1912 and, in 1913, McCay's appointment was terminated.

The outbreak of war revived his military career and, on 15 August, he was given command of the 2nd Infantry Brigade of the newly formed AIF. On arrival in Egypt, McCay established his reputation both as a conscientious trainer and as a martinet. He led his brigade to Gallipoli where it performed as well as any in the AIF, losing about half its strength in the confused fighting of the first few days. McCay himself was hit twice, although not seriously wounded. During the fighting in the British zone at Cape Helles, however, when the brigade was used to augment British troops for the attack on Krithia, McCay was wounded — this time severely. His leg was broken by a bullet and he was evacuated to Egypt. He was promoted to take command of the newly formed 2nd Division, but his damaged leg broke again and he was invalided to Malta and then home to Australia.

McCay received a hero's welcome, his temporary promotion to major general was progressed and he was made Inspector General of the AIF in Australia on 29 November 1915. By avoiding a medical board, he managed to return to the Middle East and command of the newly formed 5th Division on 22 March 1916. His initial period with his new division was not a happy experience for his officers or men as his obsession with training saw a number of unfortunate incidents, culminating in the sacking of one of his brigade commanders for a mistake that was, in fact, McCay's. However, he retained his command and took the division to France in June. A month later, he led his division to destruction in the Battle of Fromelles.

McCay's command performance during this battle has been subject to a great deal of critical analysis, much of it ill-informed or deduced from his personal reputation. He maintained his strict, almost puritanical, discipline, even sacking another brigade commander allegedly for drunkenness, although it was apparent to all that the man was exhausted.

McCay continued to command the division for several months after the battle, taking it to the Somme battlefield late in that conflict and leading it in the build-up to the battle of Fleurs. However, his enemies were catching up with him and, exploiting his continuing problems with his wounded leg, had him invalided back to England in January 1917. He never again commanded troops in battle. He remained in his administrative command until the end of the war, playing a significant part in the demobilisation and repatriation process.

McCay's military reputation never recovered. He was demobilised in 1919 and retired from the Army in 1926. He never sought to excuse or explain his actions, nor publicly defend himself against his many critics. His more famous contemporary, Sir Cyril Brudenell White, remarked that McCay was Australia's greatest soldier, greater even than Monash. Popular memory does not agree.

After many years of civil service in a number of different federal and state posts, McCay died in Melbourne on 1 October 1930. Like many generals, he unfairly bore the brunt of popular revulsion against the human cost of the war. Unlike many other generals, however, his personal character directly contributed to his unpopularity.

# BIBLIOGRAPHY

AIF Military Pamphlet, *Notes on the German Army*, Government Printer, Melbourne, n. d.

Barton, Peter, *Fromelles: A Report based upon research in the Hauptstaatsarchiv Kriegsarchiv, Munich*, Unpublished Report to the Australian Army, 2008.

Bean, C.E.W., *The Official History of Australia in the War of 1914-1918, Vol. III, The A.I.F. in France: 1916*, Angus and Robertson, Sydney, 1940.

Bidwell, Shelford and Graham, Dominick, *Fire-power: The British Army Weapons and Theories of War 1904-1945*, Pen and Sword, Barnsley, 2004.

Bond, Brian and Cave, Nigel, *Haig: A Reappraisal 70 Years On*, Leo Cooper, Barnsley, 1999.

Chappell, Mike, *The British Army in World War I (2)*, Osprey Publishing, Oxford, 2005.

Cobb, Paul, *Fromelles 1916*, Tempus, Stroud, 2007.

Corfield, Robin, *Don't Forget Me, Cobber*, Corfield and Co, Melbourne, 2000.

Cron, Hermann, *Imperial German Army 1914-18: Organisation, Structure, Orders-of-Battle*, Helion, Solihull, 2002.

Davies, Frank and Maddocks, Graham, *Bloody Red Tabs: General Officer Casualties of the Great War 1914-1918*, Leo Cooper, London, 1995.

Doughty, Robert, *Pyrrhic Victory: French Strategy and Operations in the Great War*, Belknap, Cambridge, Mass., 2005.

Ekins, Ashley, 'Fighting to exhaustion: morale, discipline and combat effectiveness in the armies of 1918' in *1918 Year of Victory*, proceedings of the Australian War Memorial Conference, Australian War Memorial, Canberra, 2008.

Ellis, John and Cox, Richard, *The World War 1 Databook: The Essential Facts and Figures for all the Combatants*, Aurum Press, London, 1993.

Fostern, D.S.V and Marrion, R.J., *The British Army 1914-18*, Osprey Publishing, Oxford, 1978.

Laparra, Jean-Claude and Hesse, Pascal, *The German Infantryman, 1914-18*, Histoire and Collections, Paris, 2008.

Lindsay, Patrick, *Fromelles*, Hardie Grant, Prahran, 2008.

McMullen, Ross, *Pompey Elliott*, Scribe, Carlton North, 2002.

Neillands, Robin, *Attrition: The Great War on the Western Front – 1916*, Robson Books, London, 2001.

Pedersen, Peter, *Fromelles*, Leo Cooper, Barnsley, 2004.

*Report upon the Department of Defence*, Government Printer, Melbourne, 1917.

Sheffield, Gary, *The Somme*, Cassell, London, 2003.

Sheffield, Gary and Bourne, John (eds), *Douglas Haig : war diaries and letters, 1914-1918*, Weidenfeld & Nicolson, London, 2005.

Simkins, Peter, *Kitchener's Army: The Raising of the New Armies, 1914-16*, Manchester University Press, Manchester, 1988.

Simkins, Peter, *The First World War: The Western Front 1914-1916*, Osprey Publishing, Oxford, 2002.

Stevenson, David, *1914-1918: The History of the First World War*, Allen Lane, London, 2004.

Sumner, Ian, *The French Army 1914-18*, Osprey Publishing, Oxford, 1995.

Sumner, Ian, *French Poilu 1914-18*, Osprey Publishing, Oxford, 2009.

Terraine, John, *Douglas Haig: The Educated Soldier*, Cassell, London, 1963.

Wilson, Brevet Major B. T., *Studies of German Defences near Lille*, Chatham, Kent, 1919.

# INDEX

203